Dramaturgy of Migration

Dramaturgy of Migration: Staging Multilingual Encounters in Contemporary Theatre examines the function of dramaturgy and the role of the dramaturg in making a theatre performance situated at the crossroads of multiple theatre forms and performative devices.

This book explores how these forms and devices are employed, challenged, experimented with, and reflected upon in the work of migrant theatre by performance and dance artists. Meerzon and Pewny ask: What impact do peoples' movement between continents, countries, cultures, and languages have on the process of meaning production in plays about migration created by migrant artists? What dramaturgical devices do migrant artists employ when they work in the context of multilingual productions, with the texts written in many languages, and when staging performances that target multicultural and multilingual theatregoers? And, finally, how do the new multilingual practices of theatre writing and performance meet and transform the existing practices of postdramatic dramaturgies? By considering these questions in a global context, the editors explore the overlapping complexities of migratory performances with both range and depth.

Ideal for scholars, students, and practitioners of theatre, dramaturgy, and devising, *Dramaturgy of Migration* expresses not only the practicalities of migratory performances but also the emotional responses of the artists who stage them.

Yana Meerzon is Professor of Theatre Studies in the Department of Theatre, University of Ottawa. She has published on theatre of exile and migration, as well as cultural and interdisciplinary studies. Her books include *A Path of the Character: Michael Chekhov's Inspired Acting and Theatre Semiotics* (2005) and *Performing Exile— Performing Self: Drama, Theatre, Film* (2012); she has also co-edited several book collections and special issues of journals on these topics.

Katharina Pewny is a Berlin-based yoga teacher and independent researcher of movement studies, who was previously Professor of Performance Studies at Ghent University. Her publications include the monograph *Das Drama des Prekären* (2011) and other publications on performance and the creation of diverse communities.

Dramaturgy of Migration

Staging Multilingual Encounters in
Contemporary Theatre

**Edited by Yana Meerzon and
Katharina Pewny**

Routledge
Taylor & Francis Group

LONDON AND NEW YORK

First published 2020
by Routledge
2 Park Square, Milton Park, Abingdon, Oxon OX14 4RN

and by Routledge
605 Third Avenue, New York, NY 10017

First issued in paperback 2021

Routledge is an imprint of the Taylor & Francis Group, an informa business

Publisher's Note
The publisher has gone to great lengths to ensure the quality of this reprint
but points out that some imperfections in the original copies may be
apparent.

British Library Cataloguing-in-Publication Data
A catalogue record for this book is available from the British Library

Library of Congress Cataloging-in-Publication Data
A catalog record for this book has been requested

ISBN 13: 978-1-03-208898-3 (pbk)
ISBN 13: 978-1-138-57628-5 (hbk)

Typeset in Times New Roman
by Apex CoVantage, LLC

Contents

Figures

Author biographies

Art Babayants is an artist-scholar exploring the phenomenology of multilingual acting and spectating, as well as the concept of multilingual dramaturgy. He has published on Canadian diasporic theatre, queer dramaturgy, applied theatre, and contemporary musical theatre. He is also the founder and artistic director of Toronto Laboratory Theatre (www. torontolab.org).

Christopher Balme holds the chair in theatre studies at Ludwig-Maximilians-University Munich. His research interests include global theatre history, theatre and institutional aesthetics, and theatre and migration.

Ana Candida Carneiro is a Brazilian-Italian playwright, translator, and scholar. She is the founder and artistic director of Babel Theater Project, a hub to make theatre at the crossroads of languages, cultures, and disciplines. She is currently a visiting artist in playwriting at Amherst College.

Indu Jain is an assistant professor of English at Delhi University, India. She is interested in probing the existing lacunae in Indian theatre historiography vis-à-vis feminist directors' contributions and their pedagogy. Her latest essay on the same topic "Feminist Processes and Performance: Interventions in Anamika Haksar's Antar Yatra" was published in *Theatre Research International*.

Jonas Hassen Khemiri is a Swedish writer, publishing novels and plays that have been translated into more than 25 languages. His debut novel, *One Eye Red* (*Ett öga rött*), was published in 2003; his plays, *Invasion!* and *I Call my Brothers* have been staged in Europe, Canada, and the United States.

Kasia Lech, with a Ph.D. from University College Dublin, lectures at Canterbury Christ Church University. Her publications focus on verse in theatre, translation, and multilingualism. Kasia trained at the Polish National Academy of Theatre Arts and performed internationally. She co-founded Polish Theatre Ireland and is an executive director at The-TheatreTimes.com.

Alvin Eng Hui Lim is an assistant professor in the Department of English Language and Literature at the National University of Singapore and Deputy Director of the Asian Shakespeare Intercultural Archive (A|S|I|A, http://a-s-i-a-web.org/). He recently published a monograph, *Digital Spirits in Religion and Media: Possession and Performance* (2018). He has also published on Singapore theatre, digital archiving, and religious performance.

Yana Meerzon, a professor at the University of Ottawa, has published on theatre of exile and migration, as well as cultural and interdisciplinary studies. Her books include *A Path of the Character: Michael Chekhov's Inspired Acting and Theatre Semiotics*, (2005) and *Performing Exile— Performing Self: Drama, Theatre, Film* (2012). She has also co-edited several book collections and special issues of journals on these topics.

Laura Paetau, dramaturg at Schauspielhaus Zürich, has been working as a dramaturg on queer-feminist and postmigrant topics, including *Frutas Afrodisíacas*, a co-production between Studio Я, Maxim Gorki Theatre, and Ballhaus Naunynstraße. She was part of the research training group Between Spaces at the Institute for Latin American Studies, Freie Universität Berlin.

Ameet Parameswaran is an Assistant Professor in Theatre and Performance Studies, School of Arts and Aesthetics, Jawaharlal Nehru University. He publishes on political theatre and performance, neoliberalism, region studies, and performance theory. His monograph, *Performance and the Political: Power and Pleasure in Contemporary Kerala* was published in 2017.

Katharina Pewny (dr. habil) is a Berlin-based teacher of inclusive yoga and a movement coach and a former professor of performance studies at Ghent University. Her publications include the monograph *Das Drama des Prekären* (2011), the edition of the *Dance Research Journal* "Work With(Out) Boundaries" (2019), and other publications on performance and the creation of diverse communities.

Judith Rudakoff is a dramaturg and scholar whose work focuses on eliciting personal narratives and developing them into autoethnographic performances. Recent books include the edited collections *Performing*

Exile: Foreign Bodies (2017) and *Performing #MeToo: How Not to Look Away* (forthcoming 2020). Rudakoff is a professor of theatre at York University in Toronto, Canada.

Alvina Ruprecht, Professor Emerita (Carleton University) and currently Adjunct Professor (University of Ottawa), was a theatre critic on national radio (CBC Ottawa) for 30 years. Research funded by The Social Sciences and Humanities Research Council of Canada (SSHRC) grants allowed her to continue her postcolonial research and publications. *Les Théâtres francophones du Pacifique-sud* (2016) is her latest book.

Azadeh Sharifi, Ludwig-Maximilians-University Munich, is a theatre researcher. Her work focuses on (post)migration and theatre in German theatre history and postcolonalism and intersectionality in contemporary European theatre. Her dissertation *Theater für Alle? Partizipation von Postmigranten am Beispiel der Bühnen der Stadt Köln* (2011) is considered essential on these topics.

Margareta Sörenson is a Swedish theatre and dance critic, journalist, and author of several books, such as *Mats Ek* (2011), as well as English-Swedish works on contemporary puppetry such as *An Even Greater Little Theatre—40 Years with Puppet Theatre Tittut* (2017). She has contributed to the *World Encyclopedia of Puppetry*, *Dictionnaire Universel des Femmes Créatrices*, and *The Performing Arts in the Nordic Countries* (published in Japan), amongst others. She is president of the International Association of Theatre Critics.

Dragan Todorovic, University of Kent, has published nine books of fiction, creative non-fiction, and essays. His primary interests are the experience of exile and interdisciplinary studies. His books include *The Book of Revenge* (2007) and *Diary of Interrupted Days* (2010). His works have been shortlisted for the Commonwealth Writers' Prize, the Amazon First Novel Award, and the British Columbia Award for Canadian Non-Fiction, and he has won the Nereus Writers' Trust Non-Fiction Prize.

Sun Weiwei (Ph.D. in progress at Research Centre S: PAM, Ghent University [Belgium]) is a lecturer at Hubei Institute of Fine Arts (Wuhan, China). Her Ph.D. is funded by the China Scholarship Council. She is an artist (artist name: Tan Tan) and researcher dedicated to intermedia, interdisciplinary, and interventionist art activities and academic subjects.

© Tan Tan (Sun Weiwei), 2018: A Pink River (performance art). Performed by Tan Tan, at the 2018 Annual Manifestation Against Sexism in Gent, Belgium. It is a performance about a "misplaced woman" who comes from China and currently lives in Belgium, who attempts to find her place as a foreign woman despite all the stereotypes and cultural misunderstandings.

Introduction

Dramaturgies of self: language, authorship, migration

Yana Meerzon and Katharina Pewny

The word *dramaturgy* most commonly refers to the composition of the play, its plot structure, themes, characters, and its aesthetic framework. In this framework, the work of a dramaturg implies providing critical reflection about the play's composition, mostly in the dramaturg's functions as a researcher (production dramaturgy) or as a consultant, an outside eye, or an observer who helps a theatre company develop a new performance text and its actions through rehearsals. Recent developments in performance practices and scholarship have shaken these binary definitions of dramaturgy. In their book *Dramaturgy and Performance* (2008), for example, Cathy Turner and Synne Behrndt argue that twenty-first-century theatre practices reflect the crisis of mimesis and demand new forms of storytelling, something that they identify as a *dramaturgy of process*: "A dramaturgy that makes us aware of the mechanisms of communication and the artificial construction of imaginary (real) worlds, even while we are moved and engaged by them" (193). Turner and Behrndt convincingly show how new dramaturgies and performance practices have renegotiated their complex relationship with mimetic and narrative representation by foregrounding their own construction and "exploring the range of ways in which 'reality' can be produced, explored and understood" (188), thus introducing a level of self-reflectivity into the practice of dramaturgy. Dramaturgy is a flexible process influenced by its social, political, and economic contexts. Turner and Behrndt further notice a shift in dramaturgy as the practice has come to focus increasingly on creating encounters between the performance and its public, between the object *seen* and the subject *seeing* (Coppens et al. 2014). They argue that more and more performances "deliberately engage with the present tense, the 'now' of live performance—less a matter of live presence than of live encounter" (202). Here, dramaturgy and performance become a process for facilitating an encounter. This process results in what Turner and Behrndt call "an open dramaturgy" that can facilitate a space of encounter for its public and an open-ended viewing experience in which the spectator becomes the major "ingredient" of what Patrice Pavis calls postdramatic or performative dramaturgies (2014: 14–39).

In an age of mass migration and postmodern aesthetic sensibilities, the borders between different performing arts (dance, theatre, and performance) and fine arts blur even further, whereas theatre and new media interweave in hybrid performances. These changes force methodological questions of performance making as well as the artists' and the audiences' focus on the construction, performance, and fundamentals of making and encountering self in and through the media of performance. This collection aims to encourage a dialogue on the function of dramaturgy and the role of the dramaturg in constructing performative encounters within the conditions of onstage and offstage multilingualism caused by the realities of global movements. The questions the book asks are as follows:

- What impact has the movement of individuals between countries, cultures, and languages produced in terms of (1) the process of production of meaning and (2) staging this divided self in the plays created by migrant artists and about migration?
- What dramaturgical devices for constructing a performative encounter in theatre do such directors as, for instance, the Berlin-based artist Jael Ronen and her ensemble (Maxim Gorki Theatre Berlin) employ when they work in the context of multilingual performance, with the texts written in many languages, and staging productions that target multicultural and multilingual theatregoers?
- And, finally, how do these new multilingual practices of theatre writing and performance meet and transform the existing practices of postdramatic dramaturgies as found in immersive, relational, durational, and other performative practices?

To begin approaching these questions, we propose a hypothesis: we argue that today's multilingual theatre practices bring forward new "dramaturgies of self" that reflect the everyday alienation experienced by both migrant theatre makers and their audiences. These dramaturgies are brought forward by forced displacement, political banishment, war threats, asylum seeking, economic migration, and personal tourism. In times of mass migration and rising nationalisms, populist political discourses and fundamentalism, theatre makers, authors, and performers who choose to speak about these issues offer their creative search for a collective better understanding of these pressing historical phenomena, as well as our relations to the stranger, the Other (Ahmed 2000). Theatre negotiates these discourses within professional polylogues of contact created by the people who make theatre performances and the audiences who come to encounter them (Pewny et al.

2014). These professional polylogues of contact present a complex web of dramaturgical relations, propositions, and choices that reflect our multicultural encounters offstage and that we propose to study in this volume. Contributions selected for this book examine multiple dramaturgical practices of multilingualism that include artists experimenting with words in many languages (practices of logos) as well as recognising multilingualism as a pluralistic concept of "languages of the stage" (Pavis 1982). Collectively, these chapters speak of the new dramaturgical devices emerging in the practices used in multilingual theatre to negotiate verbal, visual, and sound dramaturgy of the stage. The book reveals multilingual theatre's ability to stage personal journeys of migrant theatre makers and engage new performative mechanisms of constructing and reflecting their new audiences that are often themselves multilingual and multicultural. To this degree, this collection's lexical uniqueness extends beyond its themes, as it is voiced by those migrant artists who use multilingualism as their leading artistic tool. Many of this book's contributors live through the process of linguistic negotiation on a daily basis. In fact, one might say, this collection features not one, but many Englishes that reflect the dynamic and constantly evolving nature of today's English—the most common tool of cultural negotiations, conflict resolution, and peacemaking. It is a record of this linguistic plurality in the printed form.

The work on this volume began in the spring of 2016 when Yana Meerzon, Katharina Pewny, and Gunther Martens were awarded a research fellowship by the Faculty of Arts and Philosophy at Ghent University. "Migration and Multilingualism" (a special issue of the journal *Modern Drama* [N. 61.3; 2018]) presented the first part of the project, and this collection constitutes the second. Unlike "Migration and Multilingualism", which was focused only on the practices of multilingual theatre in Europe, this book proposes a more inclusive if not global point of view. In its own dramaturgy, it freely mixes voices of theatre scholars, theatre makers, and practising dramaturgs. And so, under a single cover, the book assembles scholarly articles, artistic interventions, and personal dialogues. It tackles many practical questions of multilingual theatre, including issues of translation and comprehensibility, constructing and de-constructing dialogue, and means of audience engagement. The two opening chapters, "Suppliant Guests: *Hikesia* and the Aporia of Asylum" by Christopher Balme and "We Are Who We Are Not: Language, Exile, and Nostalgia for the Self" by Dragan Todorovic, exemplify this approach. Balme focuses on the Greek concept of *hikesia*, known as granting sanctuary to strangers, which he reads against the current debates on refugees and asylum seeking in Europe. Using Derrida's discussion of language and hospitality and the Greek textual and iconographical depictions of *hikesia*, he examines Jelinek's play *Die Schutzbefohlenen* as a manifestation of the claims for political asylum as pressure on today's systems of polity. This chapter is followed by Dragan Todorovic's reflection on the processes of self-translation as practised by a polycultural artist. He demonstrates how a subject of many languages and many selves speaks and writes from the liminal space of translational encounter where languages, cultural traditions, and beliefs meet and intersect.

In its three sections, the book oscillates between these two points of reflection and experience. It builds both on theatre makers' strategies to make sense of migration through artistic practice and theatre scholars' need to investigate the historical, social, geographical, and cultural contexts that inform these practices. Part I, "On Migration and Self-Translation", features four chapters that describe and examine the work of multilingualism in the context of personal displacement offered from the perspectives of theatre makers, actors, and playwrights who are themselves in exile. Part II, "On Inter- and Intra-Multilingualism of Migration", focuses on the issues of decolonization, intracultural displacement, translational encounter, and enabling empathy through experiential writing. These case studies at some of the many dramaturgical strategies that can be used in multilingual performances dedicated to expanding the concept of multilingualism to the notion of the languages of the stage. The chapters acknowledge the multifaceted reality of today's urban practices and histories that are constantly reflected in the dramaturgy of multilingual performance. This reality shapes the artistic practices of many multilingual and pluricultural artists who also see themselves as post-migratory or even post-hybrid. Part III, "On Dramaturgy of Globalised, Transnational, and Cosmopolitan Encounters", focuses on encounter as the leading strategy of multilingual dramaturgy in the work of transnational and globalised artists whose personal nomadic position is conditioned by the circumstances of their work, including the type of performance research they do or the artistic contracts they hold; political and economic policies on migration in the countries of their residence; and other circumstances of their artistic practice. Questions of decolonising history, de- and re-constructing one's cultural and linguistic identity, phenomenological experiences, and strategies of translational multilingualism constitute the focal point of these chapters.

Thus, in its multiple takes on multilingualism and languages of the stage, the book comments on many dramaturgical aspects of making a multilingual performance, including heteroglossia, dialogicity, language dialects and use of pidgin, language accusation and loss, and issues of accents and code switching. In its thinking through the performative functions of multilingualism, such as political resistance, subverting stereotypes, (re)constructing memory, and creating utopian performances of hope (Dolan 2005), the book examines the necessary dramaturgical steps of making theatre and performance arts in an age of migration, when many transnational and migrant artists need to engage with the intercultural paradigms of performance dramaturgy and must challenge their normative habits of performance making and dissemination. We hope this book will prove useful to emerging and established theatre artists, writers, dramaturgs, literary managers, educators, and students. Our aim is to assist them in undertaking multilingualism not as a challenge but as a tool in their creative, analytical, and pedagogical work.

This collection, however, would not have evolved into its present form without the work of Lawrence Aronovitch, who spent hours reading, editing, and commenting on its chapters. Tessa Vannieuwenhuyze's support at the beginning of this project was crucial as well, whilst Aisling Murphy helped us at the final steps of this work. We would like to thank the research group THALIA (Interplay of Theatre, Literature and Media in Performance) hosted by Ghent University and the Free University of Brussels and convened by Katharina Pewny, Kornee van der Haven, and Inge Arteel for providing financial support for this work. Finally, our special thanks to Magda Romanska, the editor of the Routledge Dramaturgy series, for taking on and supporting this project.

Works cited

Ahmed, Sara. *Strange Encounters: Embodied Others in Post-Coloniality*. Routledge, 2000.

Coppens, Jeroen, et al. "Introducing Dramaturgies in the New Millennium." *Dramaturgies in the New Millennium: Relationality, Performativity and Potentiality*, edited by Katharina Pewny et al., Narr, 2014.

Dolan, Jill. *Utopia in Performance: Finding Hope at the Theater*. U of Michigan P, 2005.

Lehmann, Hans-Thies. *Postdramatic Theatre*. Translated and with an introduction by Karen Jürs-Munby, Routledge, 2006.

Pavis, Patrice. "Dramaturgy and Postdramaturgy." *Dramaturgies in the New Millennium: Relationality, Performativity and Potentiality*, edited by Katharina Pewny et al., Narr, 2014.

———. *Languages of the Stage: Essays in the Semiology of the Theatre*. Performing Arts Journal Publications, 1982.

Pewny, Katharina, et al., eds. *Dramaturgies in the New Millennium: Relationality, Performativity and Potentiality*. Narr, 2014.

Turner, Cathy, and Synne K. Behrndt. *Dramaturgy and Performance*. Palgrave Macmillan, 2008.

1 Suppliant guests

Hikesia and the aporia of asylum

Christopher Balme

In her theatrical text *Die Schutzbefohlenen*, translated by Gitti Honegger as *The Charges* (*Supplicants*), Elfriede Jelinek alludes to the drama *The Suppliant Maidens* (*Hiketes*) by Aeschylus as an associative reference for her engagement with the fate of refugees, in particular a group of refugees who occupied/sought refuge in Vienna's Votivkirche in 2011 and later the victims of the catastrophe of Lampedusa: "We have some branches here for peace, from the oil palm, no, we tore them off the olive tree" (Jelinek 1). Aeschylus's text employs a complex of motifs which enjoy unfortunate topicality: the escape across the sea is referred to repeatedly in the cho-rus passages and is also mirrored in the madness plaguing the figure of Io, mother of the daughters of Danaus, who has been driven from Greece to Egypt whence her daughters flee again back to Greece to escape marriage to their cousins. Aeschylus's drama also provides Jelinek with a second motif, which is not quite so evident. Jelinek's usage of *Die Schutzbefohlenen* in her title refers to the usual German translation of *Hiketes* as "die Schutzflehenden", those who plead for protection, an allusion to the Greek word *hikesia*, the ancient custom of hospitality and protection from perse-cution. This custom, or more precisely ritual, goes back to archaic times but attained in ancient Greece both ritual and legal form and thereby a degree of institutionalisation. By offering protection to a persecuted person outside his or her normal place of abode, *hikesia* can be regarded as a legal and ritual extension of hospitality. Supplicants, irrespective of origin and social standing—runaway slaves, debtors, criminals—were offered protection at certain sacred sites through a ritual. In the ancient law of asylum, sacred and secular law were inextricably intertwined.

This interpenetration of sacred and secular law seems to have made the theme of *hikesia* or the granting of asylum a recurrent and central question in ancient tragedy. Although we may think immediately of Antigone when discussing the clash of these two legal principles, the case of funereal rights is actually rather unusual. In 10 of the 33 surviving tragedies, *hikesia* and asylum play a central role. In two, we even have the word in the title: the plays entitled *Hiketes* by Aeschylus and Euripides share the same title but deal with completely different stories. In four tragedies, asylum seekers or supplicants play a role: apart from the already mentioned plays, we find *The Children of Hercules* by Euripides and *Oedipus at Colonus* by Sophocles, where the title character seeks asylum at the shrine of the Erinyes, the Furies. In the *Oresteia*, there is also a direct reference to *hikesia*, when Orestes seeks protection at a temple after his bloody deed.

In the following, the task will be to examine the particular dramatic and theatrical conflict potential which appears to reside in the ritual of *hikesia*. The evident tension between sacred and secular law, which was already controversial in ancient times, can be traced to the present day and still features as a basis for contemporary theatrical and philosophical figurations of asylum and refugees. In the first part of the chapter, I will examine the concept of *hikesia* as it was understood in Greek and Roman times. This will be followed by a discussion of two dramas in which *hikesia* features prominently: *The Suppliant Maidens* by Aeschylus, perhaps the ur-tragedy of *hikesia*, and *The Children of Hercules* by Euripides, read through a production of the latter by the American director Peter Sellars. In each of the European and American cities in which the play was produced, Sellars integrated refugees and asylum seekers into the performance in order to confront the polis with supplicants on their own doorstep. These examples will then be integrated into some political and philosophical observations on the fundamental structure, perhaps aporia, of the *hikesia* question. The controversial status of this law/custom will be discussed with reference to Jacques Derrida's essay on hospitality, which points out that both hospitality and hostility share a common root. This inner contradiction inherent in the notion of hospitality he encapsulates in the word *hostipitalité* (hostipitality). Then and now, political asylum places considerable pressure on the polity confronted with the dilemma of according strangers/refugees sanctuary.

Hikesia and asylum in the ancient world

Hikesia und *asylia* are two practices or institutions which individually and in combination provided protection from persecution. The former refers to a ritual, which a supplicant (*hiketes*) could carry out to obtain sanctuary. It seems that *hikesia* could be provided under two conditions. The supplicant had to carry an olive branch wrapped in wool and enter a holy place, a sanctuary, such as a temple or altar. As long as the supplicant retained direct contact with this place he or she was protected by law and by the relevant deity. *Hikesia* could also be performed if a person embraced the knee or touched the chin of another person.

If one understands *hikesia* as a ritual that must be performed to be efficacious, then the result is a changed status of the person in question: the person
now finds him or herself in the state of *asylos*. This status is the prerequisite
for the institution of asylum. The Greek word *asylia* (ἀσυλία) means invio-
lability or invulnerability and was used in several contexts: it guaranteed
the safety of important persons, such as emissaries or messengers, but also
athletes on the way to the Olympic Games and even actors who had to
participate in the Dionysian festivals. In a second narrower meaning, *asylia*
was understood as the right to protection from persecution. This in turn
was connected to a particular place, the *asylon*, the aforesaid sanctuary or
temple. The degree of protection, however, was not necessarily the same for
all sacred places. For the Greeks, the controversial question was the degree
to which *asylia* had a recognisable legal status. Some temples only had local
recognition; others, such as certain temples of Athena and Poseidon, pos-
sessed transregional status. Whatever the status, there was general acceptance that at such sacred places, worldly laws had no purchase: the runaway
slave, the debtor, or common criminal, all those who performed *hikesia*,
were outside the domain of normal jurisdiction. It is this central moment of
tension and conflict which motivated not only the Greek tragedians but also
in its current manifestation as church asylum has remained efficacious and
controversial until the present.[1]

The ritual of *hikesia* had a number of theatrical aspects as it had both a
spatial and a corporeal dimension. In her study *Das Drama der Hikesie:
Ritual und Rhetorik in Aischylos' Hikesie*, Susanne Gödde shows that the
specific effect of *hikesia* was based on the fact that Greek religion was characterised by a pronounced consciousness for the sacred character of places,
which stood in a particular relationship to the gods (27). Within such places,
the supplicant was safe from persecution, because to enter such a space to
remove, arrest, or even kill the *hiketes* would inevitably mean incurring the
wrath of the local deity. The sacred space was defined by its demarcation
from the everyday world by means of separating off a certain section from
everyday space. The notion of sacrality, which implies also spatial delimita-
tion, is contained in the etymology of the word "temple". It goes back to the
term *templum* (Greek τέμευος) and the root τεμ, meaning "to cut" (Cassirer
100). The current practice of religious asylum is based on such an understanding of the *templum* which draws its legal justification from Roman
law. It is more an ancient practice than a legal principle. As with current
cases of church asylum, the goal of *hikesia* in ancient times was not only
to obtain temporary protection but also often to gain access to the country
or polis. This required, however, a second step – namely, application to the
political leader of the polis (Gödde 28).

The second variation of the ritual is corporeal or gestural in nature
and requires that the supplicant touch the supplicated person. This was

performed most commonly by embracing the knees, but touching the chin was also possible. This form of special ritual embrace or touching provided a similar degree of protection. For example, in *The Suppliant Women* by Euripides, the women implore Theseus to grant them protection by referring directly to this ritual: "By thy beard, kind friend, glory of Hellas, I do beseech thee, as I clasp thy knees and hands in my misery" (195). The gesture of embracing the knees is something we associate today with a gesture of extreme submissiveness. That is implied by the word supplication, which derives in turn from the Latin *supplicō* or *supplicium*. The practice is well documented in iconographic sources, which suggests that in ancient times, *hikesia* was part of a generally comprehensible cultural and visual code.

A common iconographic motif is Cassandra's abduction and rape by Ajax the Locrian, who has sought refuge in the Temple of Athena in Troy after the city's conquest by the Greeks. In one representation (Figure 1.1),

Figure 1.1 Ajax abducting Cassandra who is embracing a statue of Athena. Red-figured calyx crater

Credit: Museo Archeologico Nazionale, Naples, 82923

Ajax pursues Cassandra with sword in hand and seizes her even though she is embracing a statue of the goddess. According to the myth, the rape of Cassandra also constituted a desecration of the temple and resulted in various catastrophes for the Greeks during their return from Troy.

Another version of the myth (Figure 1.2) is represented on a red-figured crater from Paestum and which dates to around 350 BC. The image shows a similar situation, but the roles are reversed. It is Ajax who is embracing Athena and seeking sanctuary. On the right, a figure, probably a priestess, is trying to flee. The masks suggest that this is a theatrical representation, perhaps referring to a satyr play. The gesture of embrace, however, is unambiguous.

The configuration of holy place and performed gesture leads finally to the acceptance but not necessarily the incorporation of the supplicant into the new community. This next stage of the ritual distinguishes *hikesia* from other practices of hospitality, which by definition were only granted temporarily. In this final stage of *hikesia* lies the greatest potential for conflict because it implies a permanent incorporation into the polis, the granting of citizenship so to speak. Religious historian Jochen Derlien has drawn attention to this aspect of the practice with explicit reference to *The Children of Hercules* and to *The Supplicant Maidens* by Aeschylus: "Through the ritual of supplication (*hikesia*) as part of the hospitality performed at a local sanctuary, temporary asylum could be obtained and then subsequently

Figure 1.2 Ajax embracing statue of Athena. Red-figured volute crater

Credit: Museo Nazionale Etrusco di Villa Giulia, Rome, Inventory: 50279 (1. Inv.)

permanent citizen status in a foreign state (μετοικία/κατοικία, *metoikia/ katoikia*) (Eurip. Heraclidae; Aisch. Hiketides)" (865). The refugee could under certain circumstances become a *metic*, a resident alien, someone who is more than a foreigner (*xenoi*) but not a full member of the polis.[2]

In order to understand what conflict and tension such a practice potentially entailed, we shall now turn to two works whose stories provide the clearest exposition of *hikesia* as a model of dramatic conflict. In this recurrent motif of Greek tragedy, a political problem is played out that evidently posed an almost insoluble problem for the Greek body politic.

Hiketiden and *Herakliden*: on the limits of hospitality

In *The Suppliant Maidens* by Aeschylus, the 50 daughters of Danaus flee from Egypt with their father across the sea to Argos in order to escape forced marriage with their cousins. Arriving on the coast, they seek sanctuary at the birthplace of their mother, Io, who was transformed by Zeus into a cow. They enter a sacred grove near the city of Argos holding olive branches wrapped in wool. They form the chorus and reflect on their own actions:

> To what kinder land could we turn than this,
> with our suppliant olive branches,
> handheld implements wreathed in wool?
> $(18–20)^3$

Danaus draws attention to the place as a sanctuary by explaining to his daughters the significance of the Grove:

> Quickly, come here now,
> with white-wreathed suppliant branches solemnly
> held in the left hand, emblem of august Zeus
> . . .

And, in what will become a recurrent theme in the play, he notes the correct comportment required there:

> Let nothing bold
> attend your voice, and nothing vain come forth
> in glance but modesty and reverence.
> (191–199)

After performing the necessary rites, the ritual of *hikesia* is completed and protection is granted. But as the admonitions of Danaus suggest, the ritual is based on the principle of reciprocity: sanctuary in exchange for reverential, even submissive behaviour.

The actual drama begins with the entrance of Pelasgus, the King of Argos. In his first speech, he adumbrates not only the conflict of this drama but also the drama of refugees in general:

> Whence come this crowd of barbarians?
> What shall we call you? So outlandishly
> Arrayed in this exotic luxury
> of robes and headbands, not in Argive fashion
> nor even in Greek?
>
> (234–240)

Pelasgus articulates the age-old prejudices besetting encounters between strangers and hosts. *Hikesia* implies an almost invariable engagement with strangers, perhaps even exotic peoples, and, therefore, poses an eternal ethical challenge, even when the rites have been performed, in this case the correct use of the olive branches. Only after the genealogy of the daughters has been explained does the king understand where they come from and that the strangers are actually originally Greek. He has less sympathy for the motivations behind their flight, the desire to escape incestuous marriages: marriage between relatives is normal in Egypt and, therefore, the legal appeal of the daughters is shaky, Pelasgus remarks. He claims that such ties might even strengthen kinship: "Thus greater grows the strength of human families" (339). The dilemma for the king is of a different kind. Is he prepared—should he grant asylum—to risk war with the Egyptians? The decision is a difficult one, because by handing the daughters over to the Egyptians, he risks contravening *hikesia* and the laws of hospitality. This would mean incurring divine wrath. Pelasgus has only bad options. He, therefore, urges the daughters to resolve the conflict according to the laws of Egypt:

> If Egyptus' sons have power over you
> by your city's laws, claiming they are nearest
> of kin, who would wish in that to oppose them?
> You must plead your case according to your laws
> at home, that they lack authority over you.
>
> (387–391)

The debate that follows between Pelasgus and the chorus weighs the rights of the supplicants against the responsibility of the ruler for his people. Pelasgus then leaves to explain the situation to the polis, deferring the final decision to the people. In his speech, which is reported by Danaus, Pelasgus argues that the daughters should be granted asylum so as not to provoke the anger of Zeus. The resulting vote brings a clear decision: the daughters are accepted into Argos, making the decision legally binding.

The conflict gains in intensity with the arrival of the Egyptians, represented by a messenger, because there is now a real danger of war. They are about to remove the daughters by force, and only the second appearance of Pelasgus is able to defuse the situation:

> You there! What are you doing? By what arrogance
> dare you insult this land of Pelasgian men?
> Do you think you have come to a woman's land? You are
> barbarians, and you trifle insolently
> With Greeks.
>
> (911–915)

The Egyptian messenger withdraws but not without threatening war and revenge. The play ends with some general aphorisms regarding the plight of strangers and refugees. Once more, Danaus admonishes the daughters to behave properly in their new home:

> Time becomes the touchstone of the stranger,
> An immigrant group in a foreign land, which bears
> The brunt of every evil tongue, and is
> The easy target of calumny. I beg
> you not to bring me shame.
>
> (993–996)

The play ends on a positive note; the catastrophe has been averted for the time being. This is, however, only a temporary respite, because in the second play of the tetralogy—*The Egyptians*, which has not survived—the daughters are abducted and forced into marriage, which then results in the infamous murder of the 50 husbands. Although Zeus is the final arbiter in this conflict, the realisation dawns that such a decision always implies both weighing choices and balancing competing interests in legal terms between religious and secular imperatives. The long debates in the play focus on the challenges that *hikesia* implies for the commonweal. As simple as the ritual may be to perform—extending an olive branch wrapped in wool—the political implications are often too complex to be resolved satisfactorily.

We find a similar dilemma in *The Children of Hercules* by Euripides. We are once again in Argos, where a powerful king, Eurystheus, is determined to kill the children of the dead hero Heracles. Wherever they seek refuge, Eurystheus threatens the city with attack, and they are denied sanctuary until they come to the temple of Zeus at Marathon in Attica. In Athens, represented by the king and son of Theseus, Demophon, they find a polis resolute enough to defy Eurystheus and to take *hikesia* seriously. It is not necessary to explicate the action of the play except to note that the performance of the ritual of *hikesia* marks the beginning of the play. A messenger from the king tries to abduct the children forcibly, even though they are in a sanctuary and the necessary ritual has been performed. The children's protector, the old man Iolaos, calls out that *hikesia* is about to be violated:

> All you who live in Athens, longtime residents,
> Help us! We're here as suppliants of Zeus,
> The Guardian of the Meeting Place, and yet
> We're being attacked and our garlands desecrated,
> An insult to the city and an affront to the gods!
>
> (Euripides 69–74)

The male children of Hercules are onstage in full view of the audience, whilst the daughters are being protected inside the temple by Alcmene and are concealed from public view. Whilst the male children are visible, they are also silent. It is not until the daughter Macaria offers herself up for sacrifice that the children are given a voice.

The theatrical representation of *hikesia* as refugee children needing protection forms the central idea behind Peter Sellars's production of the play. Between 2002 and 2007, he staged the play several times in different countries in protest against the way refugees were being treated. Although the production had several iterations, the basic structure remained the same. In the version staged in Amsterdam in 2004, the *mise en scène* of the Euripides play was framed by a public discussion between refugee experts and a member of the local council for refugees on the one hand and a post-performance discussion with the audience on the other. During the actual performance, a chorus consisting of young refugees sat onstage and gazed at the audience. In some versions of the evening, post-performance discussions finished with a meal in a nearby restaurant. In the American production at the American Repertory Theatre, there was also an additional programme with documentary films about the countries of origin of the refugees. In interviews, Sellars stressed repeatedly how theatre and democracy were intricately and archetypically connected in ancient Greece. He argued that theatre then was seen as an extension of and even an improvement on the democratic process. All Greek tragedies, he claimed, deal with foreigners, women, or children – i.e., with those persons who are actually excluded from the theatre and political assemblies. Although most reviews engaged with the ethical implications of using this kind of authentic "material", there is another ethical question which is equally significant but less often reflected on. This concerns the responsibility of the city or state in question to accommodate refugee children. Most critical discourse focused on the production but not on the wider political implications behind it.

In Holland, the young refugees were about to be repatriated and their camp closed. Their presence onstage posed the question of *hikesia* with particular urgency. In an interview given for Dutch television, Sellars drew explicit parallels between the wider democratic principles motivating the play and the particular political situation pertaining in Europe:

> For me, it's about creating this shared space in democracy where instead of thinking about people and looking at them you talk with them and where instead of having a mass of virtual people on television or statistics in a political debate, there is a human being in the room with them, and you realise that every human being is here, has a right to exist, and this actually is an amazing set of possibilities, and in the case of most of the refugees and most of these immigrants, these are the most heroic people on the planet! I mean, if somebody has made it here from Afghanistan, they are survivors; they are resourceful; they are motivated. And so the disaster of the laws which are now in place in the European Union *is* that these are exactly the people who are not allowed to work.
>
> (Sellars 2004)

Of course, the solution is by no means simple. In the same interview, Sellars was asked, "Are you an artist or an activist?" The mutual exclusivity implied by the question suggests that theatre must decide between two options. In Sellars's production, the spectator can switch between at least three roles: the curious listener (introductory public discussion), the aesthetic spectator (performance of the play), and the active discussant (post-performance discussion). The production thereby combines different discursive modes to engage with the political question of refugees. Since the production does not only restrict itself simply to a performance of the play but also integrates other discursive forms—expert discussion as well as questions from the audience—a dialogic mode is developed, enabling a form of direct ethical encounter that can be seen as an alternative to the representational logics of the mass media and their often highly degrading visual vocabulary (e.g., anonymous masses of refugees in orange lifejackets).

Both the play itself and the production focus on the aporia of *hikesia* understood as a dilemma that the religious and/or ethical imperative of hospitality brings with it. This aporia has been analysed by Jacques Derrida in his writings on hospitality.

Derrida on hospitality

In an essay published in 1999 with the title "Hostipitalité", Jacques Derrida expands on his ideas concerning hospitality and cosmopolitanism which played a central role in his thinking during the 1990s.[4] The somewhat oxymoronic title of the chapter is, of course, intended as he is concerned with excavating the aporia underlying the concept of hospitality which he sees as being both etymologically and philosophically founded: in French, the word *hôte* means both host and guest. As Derrida argues, it, therefore, contains an internal contradiction inasmuch as the word consists of inherent antinomies.

Derrida develops his argument from Kant's essay "Perpetual Peace" (1795), in particular from the third definitive article where Kant formulates the idea of world citizenship or cosmopolitan right:

> We speaking here, as in the previous articles, not of philanthropy, but of right; and in this sphere hospitality (*Hospitalität*) signifies the claim of a stranger entering foreign territory to be treated by its owner without hostility. The latter may send him away again, if this can be done without causing his death; but, so long as he conducts himself peaceably, he must not be treated as an enemy.
>
> (137–138)

In this famous passage, Kant formulates a global perspective when he defines world citizenship as a right of visitation (*Besuchsrecht*) in contrast to mere hospitality: "This right to present themselves to society belongs to all mankind in virtue of our *common right of possession* on the surface of the earth," on which, "as it is a globe, we cannot be infinitely scattered" (emphasis added). Derrida is less interested in discussing the notion of "world citizenship" than in Kant's use of the unusual word: *Hospitalität*. It is, Derrida explains, a word of Latin origin which contains within itself an internal contradiction, hosting as it does its own antithesis, hostility, as a kind of parasite. Hospitality embodies thereby a self-contradiction. Through the common root in the Latin word *hospes* (host but also guest or stranger) and *hostis* (a stranger or enemy) an ambivalence is established between host and guest. From the self-contradiction of the word itself, which can imply both amity and hostility, parallels can be traced to Greek tragedy and the practice of *hikesia*. The etymological kinship between *hospitalité* and *hostilité* points in turn, so Derrida argues, to hospitality as a form of power which is marked by the threshold of the house:

> [These words] belong to the current lexicon or the common semantics of hospitality, of all pre-comprehension of what "hospitality" is

and means, namely, to "welcome," "accept," "invite," "receive," "bid" someone welcome "to one's home," where, in one's own home, one is master of the household, master of the city, or master of the nation, the language, or the state, places from which one bids the other welcome (but what is a "welcome"?) and grants him a kind of right of asylum by authorizing him to cross a threshold that would be a threshold, (a door that would be a door,) a threshold that is determinable because it is self-identical and indivisible, a threshold the line of which can be traced (the door of a house, human household, family or house of god, temple or general hospital [*hôtel-dieu*], hospice, hospital or poor-house [*hôpital ou hôtel hospitalier*], frontier of a city, or a country, or a language, etc.).

(6)

Of central importance for Derrida is the idea that the host is always a ruler, whether over a home or a nation. The extension of hospitality always proceeds on the basis of a clearly demarcated power relationship regulated by law – namely, that the guest must submit himself to this law. The physical border between guest and host is, therefore, this threshold, which can take on a multiplicity of forms: the door to the house or the border of a nation-state. Above all, Derrida is concerned with the ambivalence which is not only inherent in the French word *hôte* but also which always resides in the various cultural functions of the two roles.

Conclusion

The somewhat unstable roles of host/ruler versus guest/enemy feature repeatedly in Greek tragedies. Analogous to the ambivalence analysed by Derrida, which he derives from the etymology of the word hospitality, we find an oscillating perspective on the supplicants, who are always seen as a threat if not explicitly as a direct enemy. Even if the guests do not pose a direct threat for the host, their very presence implies danger and enmity. For this reason, the whole process of accepting the supplicants plays an important role in both plays discussed. In both cases, acceptance has to be legitimised democratically by a vote. Thus the sacred right of *hikesia* is only the beginning of a process which must finally be completed in profane secular terms.

Hikesia brings into relief the ambivalence of host and guest, of asylum seeker and asylum granter, that Derrida deconstructs. The current dilemma of hospitality and asylum differs from the Greek model only in nuances and in the degree of juridification that has accrued around it. The simple Article 16a of the German constitution—"Persons persecuted on political grounds shall have the right of asylum"—has its legal "explication" in an asylum law comprising 89 paragraphs.

The basic conflict between the equally justifiable claims of secular and divine law, between the excessive demands placed on the local community by taking in strangers, and the requirement to fulfil the demands of religious custom or ethical-moral requirements remain largely unchanged. The historical and ethical obligation to grant sanctuary to the persecuted reaches its limits in the double senses, both political and physical: Argos is with us today at the shipwreck off Lampedusa as well as the electric fences of Melilla. And so the final sentence in Jelinek's text, *The Charges*, reads, "That justice will be done for us, we pray for that, may it be the fulfillment of my prayer for safe conduct, for a better lot. But it will not happen. It will not be" (Jelinek 82).

Notes

1 The extent to which church asylum is recognised legally in different jurisdictions varies greatly. In Germany, for example, it has no legal status but enjoys a kind of de facto acceptance which means that authorities are usually loath to evict or arrest asylum seekers. See www.infomigrants.net/en/post/8049/church-asylum-in-germany.
2 For a discussion of *metoikia* as a liminal state for foreigners given semi-citizen status, see David Whitehead. *The Ideology of the Athenian Metic.* Cambridge Philological Society, 1977.
3 All quotations are from *Complete Greek Tragedies.* Verse numbers will be given after the quotation.
4 See, above all, Jacques Derrida, *Of Hospitality.* Stanford, 2000.

Works cited

"asylia." *A Dictionary of Greek and Roman Antiquities*, 1890, www.perseus.tufts. edu.
Cassirer, Ernst. *The Philosophy of Symbolic Forms, Vol. 2, Mythical Thought.* Translated by Ralph Mannheim, Yale UP, 1955.
Chaniotis, Angelos. "Die Entwicklung der griechischen Asylie: Ritualdynamik und die Grenzen des Rechtsvergleichs." *Gesetzgebung in antiken Gesellschaften. Israel, Griechenland, Rom*, edited by Leonhard Burckhardt, Klaus Seybold and Jürgen von Ungern Sternberg, De Gruyter, 2007, pp. 233–246.
The Complete Greek Tragedies. Aeschylus I. Edited by Grene, David and Richard Lattimore, translated by Seth Bernardete, 3rd ed., The U of Chicago P, 2013.
Derlien, Jochen. "Asyl." *Religion in Geschichte und Gegenwart*, edited by Hans Dieter Betz, 4th Rev. ed., Mohr Siebeck, 1998, p. 865.
Derrida, Jacques. "Hostipitality." *Angelaki: Journal of the Theoretical Humanities*, translated by Barry Stocker with Forbes Morlock, vol. 5, no. 3, 2000, pp. 3–18.

Euripides. *The Plays of Euripides: The Suppliants*. Translated by E.P. Coleridge, Bell & Sons, 1910.

Gödde, Susanne. *Das Drama der Hikesie: Ritual und Rhetorik in Aischylos' Hikesie*. Aschendorff, 2000.

Gould, John. "Hiketeia." *The Journal of Hellenic Studies*, vol. 93, 1973, pp. 74–103.

Jelinek, Elfriede. *Charges (The Supplicants)*. Translated by Gitta Honegger, Seagull Books, 2016 [2013].

Kant, Immanuel. *Perpetual Peace: A Philosophical Essay*. Translated by M. Campbell Smith, Swan Sonnenschein, 1903, pp. 137–138, https://ia801406.us.archive.org/1/items/perpetualpeacea00kantgoog/perpetualpeacea00kantgoog.pdf.

Sellars, Peter. Interview. 30 May 2004, www.vpro.nl/programma/ram/afleveringen/17018915/items/17716422/. Accessed 24 Jan. 2013.

2   We are who we are not

Language, exile, and nostalgia for the self

Dragan Todorovic

1: Alchemy and panic

"Do you have a copy in Serbian?" No, I did not. The book about my life in the motherland was not written in my mother tongue. I needed distance to see things more clearly. To be 7,000 kilometres away had not been enough. When I added another language to the distance, it all came into focus.

My memoir *The Book of Revenge: A Blues for Yugoslavia* was originally published in Canada. A year later, it was awarded the Nereus Writers' Trust Non-Fiction Prize and shortlisted for another major award, and publishers in my homeland, Serbia, became interested. The book had to be translated from a foreign language which was not foreign anymore back into my mother tongue in which it was never written.

In the following months, the translator sent me a few inquiries, but nothing major: she was fine with my text and was making steady progress. I was looking forward to reading her interpretation: translation is an alchemical encounter.

Finally, the file with the translated manuscript arrived, I opened it, and after reading only a few lines, panic hit me—deep, horrible, urgent panic. Someone had stolen my whole life and written *their* book from it. The facts were there, but my whole experience had been described from another brain. I had nothing left.

2: Nostalgia for culture

Before leaving Serbia, I had published four books, written and directed a series of radio plays and two documentaries, and published enough articles to develop and polish my own recognisable style. Since that style was based on elliptical sentences and deadpan humour, it did not rely on language, and I was fairly certain it would survive translation. But there was none of my style in the manuscript on my screen. Nobody would remember me in this book.

Why was it so important for me to be recognised as *that* writer? Did I want to return via my pages into the space I once had had but then had lost? Svetlana Boym writes,

> The word nostalgia comes from two Greek roots—nostos (home) and algia (longing)—yet this composite word did not originate in ancient Greece. It is only pseudo-Greek, or nostalgically Greek. The nostalgic disorder was first diagnosed by seventeenth-century Swiss doctors and detected in mercenary soldiers[. . .]. This contagious modern disease of homesickness—*la maladie du pays*—was treated in a seventeenth-century scientific manner with leeches, hypnotic emulsions, opium, and a trip to the Alps. Nostalgia was not regarded as destiny, nor as part of the human condition, but only as a passing malaise. In the nineteenth century, the geographic longing was superseded by the historical one; *maladie du pays* turned into *mal du siécle*, but the two ailments shared many symptoms.
>
> (Boym 241)

Home ceases to exist after one goes into exile. Collective memory is adjusted so the space emptied by the exile's departure can be closed as soon as possible. The two nostalgias annihilate each other. If *la maladie du pays* is the right diagnosis, then we are longing for an a historic place; if *mal du siécle* exists, if we could somehow return to the specific time, we would find the geography impossible. Both ideas are utopian. But neither of these notions mentions the concept of *cultural nostalgia*: longing to return to the cultural milieu the individual once inhabited.

The Book of Revenge in translation had made me a foreigner in my own language. What I felt when reading it was nostalgia for my old self.

***

My first job after arriving to Canada was as a programme director at a radio station in North York. My English was progressing, but when forced to speak it for long stretches of time, I found the experience tiring. Soon, I developed terrible migraines. The attacks started around noon and by the afternoon reached punishing levels, only to abate in the evening and completely disappear during the night.

One day, with the pain being impossible to withstand, I left the office and hid in a remote corner of a poorly visited cafe with a coffee and a book. By pure chance, it was a book written in my mother tongue.

In a little while, my headache was gone. I repeated the process the next day, with the same result. Thinking it was impossible that the book had helped—surely my organism had found a bypass!—I did not bring the volume with me on the third day, only to experience new levels of pain. After that, I always carried something written in my mother tongue. Until, perhaps seven or eight months later, the migraines stopped altogether—long exposure to my second language did not hurt me anymore.

Nostalgia for culture is perhaps the strongest form of nostalgia. It can have a physical side to it—pain!—but it is cured by a simple incision of the formative language into the reformative years of early exile.

It is entirely possible that the mother tongue cures by bringing back, temporarily, habituation, which, as we know, "devours work, clothes, furniture, one's wife, and the fear of war" (Shklovsky). Perhaps this temporary blindness is needed when the speed of discovery becomes too large for comfort.

3: The diesel language of levitating individuals

An exile is a person living away from his or her native country, either by choice or because of a threat. The Office of the United Nations High Commissioner for Refugees (UNHCR) and other humanitarian organisations track only those who have been under threat—refugees and asylum seekers. Those who leave their homelands less dramatically through other channels to restart their lives somewhere far—they are not accounted for.

Almost all my friends who are exiles belong in this grey zone. Our lives were not necessarily threatened back there, wherever that was—Serbia, Syria, Siberia—nor did we exit seeking artistic challenges; we were squeezed out. We were able to apply for papers, to leave quietly, and to arrive unnoticed. Compared to the unlucky ones who had to run for their lives, who ended up in refugee camps, immigration camps, concentration camps—we are well-off. We have brought some of our belongings with us. We have photo albums, notebooks, yellowing love letters, samples of our previous works; we have interesting resumes and—most importantly—we can travel back, at least clandestinely. We are the aristocracy of *les misérables*.

This is how this "aristocrat" looks to Salman Rushdie:

> Who is he? An exile. Which must not be confused with, allowed to run into, all the other words that people throw around: émigré, expatriate, refugee, immigrant, silence, cunning. Exile is a dream of glorious return. Exile is a vision of revolution: Elba, not St Helena. It is an endless paradox: looking forward by always looking back. The exile is a ball hurled high into the air. He hangs there, frozen in time, translated into a photograph; denied motion, suspended impossibly above his native earth, he awaits the inevitable moment at which the photograph must begin to move, and the earth reclaim its own.
>
> (Rushdie 244)

This levitating individual, this dreamer, this revolutionary is never safe, no matter above what ground he is frozen. Rushdie himself was forced to become an exile after writing the *Verses*: he was protected by the state, hidden in safe places under the watchful eye of the British intelligence—still not safe. Not because of the fatwa, but because exiles and safety do not inhabit the same sentences.

Everything we exiles have is portable: a world in two suitcases. Look carefully: we are a visible minority, even where we should not be, because we walk with our eyes down. We expect no one familiar on these foreign streets; the merchandise in the windows is beyond reach—we have no reason to look up. Listen: we are an audible minority. Even later, much later, when our shoulders straighten and our look is horizontal again, one can hear the otherness in our speech. Even the best amongst us are like diesel engines—under the rich vocabulary and the proper grammar, always that hum betraying a second language, that constant tremor of accent.

4: Hiding in foreign languages

Why have I abandoned my mother tongue as a writing tool? And when I did it, what was gone with it?

Edward Sapir, one of the fathers of modern linguistics, claimed that the territory of language covered much more than the area on the map it occupied:

> Human beings do not live in the objective world alone, nor alone in the world of social activity as ordinarily understood, but are very much at the mercy of the particular language which has become the medium of expression for their society. [. . .] The fact of the matter is that the 'real world' is to a large extent unconsciously built up on the language habits of the group.
> (Sapir in Whorf 443)

Beckett, Nabokov, Conrad, Kundera, Jhumpa Lahiri, and many other authors have all abandoned their mother tongue at some point in their careers. In some cases, it is possible to explain their decisions by political means (for Nabokov, English was a shelter from the system), or as what Harold Bloom called an "anxiety of influence"—that writers create by trying to "get outside" the influence of others before them (was Beckett running away from Joyce by leaving Joyce's language?). In some other situations, it might be that creators are seeking a different vision of the world they are attempting to interpret. Beckett complained in his letters that he perceived English as a veil that had to be torn apart. Lahiri says, "In Italian I write without style, in a primitive way" (2016).

Is the escape from the mother tongue a run towards creative freedom? If we enter the territory of a language where we are not fluent and—important!—where we are acknowledged as Other and so left to roam through grammar and syntax, does that allow us authors to experiment with wild abandonment in a way that would be dangerous if we did it in our native tongue?

***

Voluntary attrition of language seems counterintuitive for someone who depends on vocabulary, but imposing restrictions on the creative process has repeatedly proven to be productive. From Django Reinhardt's burned fingers to Picasso's blue phase to béton brut of the New Brutalists to the "primitive" writing of Lahiri . . . having less material to work with bears new ideas as the brain negotiates its strategy around the limitation. Language is the stage on which that negotiation happens.

We learn languages to hide into them. They are foreign cities. When we do not (yet) have the language, we do not have the keys to the gate; we stand exposed. A mother tongue is deep, secretive, exciting. Oaths taken in the mother tongue are meaningful, secrets are taken seriously, feelings expressed with caution. In an acquired language, everything is cheaper, paler . . . shallower. Insults don't insult; promises can be broken; feelings are expressed recklessly and with abandon. In an acquired language, we behave like actors. We lend our bodies to a text that is not ours. We are who we are not.

5: Performing exile

When I came to Canada as an exile, I quickly realised I had a problem with my English. It was not my vocabulary or my spelling, but the finesse and the context. The sentences I used, the syntax, the tone—all came from Hollywood movies and rock and roll: brutal, shortcut constructions.

At the time, I was thinking in Serbo-Croatian and translating whilst talking, but that did not work for two reasons: either this process was slow, and by the time I had my precise meaning translated into English, the conversation had shifted in some other direction, or I would come up with a quick construction that only the most benevolent person cared to decipher.

One day, I was walking past a church with a Canadian friend, and she started talking about the architecture of the building. Whilst I wanted to say a few things about how I liked the bell gable, the Gothic details on the arch at the entrance, and how beautifully different the church looked amongst the demoralising Brutalist business behemoths besieging it, all I could squeeze out was, "Yeah, cool."

The construction of that eloquent sentence was only part of the problem: there was also the cadence of my English. Language is acquired with its sound, and the melodies I had picked from pop media were harsh and aggressive, presenting me in a very different light. Somewhere in the process of adopting English, I had lost my identity.

Playwright Peter Shaffer illustrates this kind of language:

> The cinema is a worrying medium for the stage playwright to work in. Its unverbal essence offers difficulties to anyone living largely by the spoken word. Increasingly, as American films grow ever more popular around the world, it is apparent that the most successful are being spoken in Screen-speak, a kind of cinematic esperanto [sic!] equally comprehensible in Bogotá and Bulawayo. For example, dialogue in heavy-action pictures, horrific or intergalactic, now consists almost entirely of the alternation of two single words—a cry and a whisper— needing translation nowhere on the planet: "Lessgidowaheer!" and "Omygaad!"
>
> (Shaffer 108)

Acquired meaning is superficial. Sound puts words into context, but the deeper shades of expression are not learned. I responded the way that action heroes would have done in one of their roles. In Serbo-Croatian, I was a connoisseur of arts; in my newly acquired language, I was an American cop. Only in my language was I smart.

***

Lingua franca is also known as *bridge* language, the linguistic zone where strangers meet occasionally for trading or border control or in passing or for negotiations. If this language seems better suited for counting goods and writing IOUs than for poetry, that is because its first role is to sustain peaceful coexistence. Was my mutilated sentence an example of bridge language? It did serve to further the communication, but if it was nothing more than the equivalent of a grunt, a confirmation I was alive and listening—hence, yes, it was a lingua franca sentence, and, yes, it distorted my identity. Does lingua franca like any other cure have side effects?

The reduction of language Shaffer writes about brings about a change of identity in life as it does in the movies. The person communicating in bridge language is hidden from view and a representative is inserted instead. Language is only part of identity, but it is impossible to speak Screenspeak without becoming a *Screenperson*.

***

In every language, certain rules are unwritten. They remain fluid, affected by history, social factors, economy, ideology. This set of standards remains mostly out of reach for an exile.

For example, in English, adjectives must follow this order: opinion-size-age-shape-colour-origin-material-purpose noun. Hence a "lovely little old rectangular green French silver whittling knife" (Forsyth). This rule is impossible to pick through conversation, and the author of the article from which this sentence was taken, Mark Forsyth, claims that the majority of native speakers of English are not even aware of this order. An exile has no access to this kind of deep knowledge and is destined to remain sounding foreign. Yoda, the popular character from the *Star Wars* saga, is not Other because he is green, two feet tall, has only three fingers, strange prickly ears, can levitate, and has been alive a few hundred years—but because he speaks his words in the wrong order.

***

Rethinking my own strategies of approaching connections between exile, language, and identity, I started working on an essay about the process of acquiring a foreign language. The issue being tightly related to sound, I decided to create an amalgamation of radio play/aural essay—I wanted to sound the depth of what I could not say. I already had the title: it was my quiet mantra, something I repeated every time I blurted out a lingua franca sentence—"In my language I am smart".

The main purpose of my play/essay was to replicate negotiations on the bridge between two languages meeting inside exile's mind. However, I was surprised to discover that the process happening there was more complicated than the imagined tug-of-war game. When I started writing the script for *In My Language I Am Smart*, the method quickly turned into an affair of permanent reduction. Yes, in the meantime, CBC Radio One had commissioned the play/essay, and this had imposed limitations in length, but that was not the reason. It became obvious that the process of negotiation between different languages unfolds through attrition. We abandon certain areas of language not because we forget the words, but because they are deemed unnecessary in the new situation. We travel light when we travel through language.

The narrative had two parallel structures: the frontal flow in which a lonely explorer is crossing the Ocean of Language and a background layer combining the words acquired with the words abandoned in the process. I wrote the primary layer entirely in the manner of solo performance: here is an individual telling his story which, although metaphorical, is rather straightforward. The secondary, essayistic layer was about the attrition of language: what is lost and what is gained (and how) in the switch between languages? It was an experiment based on techniques of vocal coaching. My aim was to have one language spoken *in front* of the body (something akin to the Victorian sound in English), whilst another was spoken from *inside* the body (as in modern American English). To achieve this, I used soft words from Serbo-Croatian and juxtaposed them with newly acquired English words. This technique did produce the feeling I was looking for: winning and losing was bundled into one. The number of layers I used whilst mixing the final version is telling: 69 stereo channels of conflicting sounds were needed to express the complexity of this settlement. The Beatles used eight.

***

Why is performing exile such a complex process?

The act of leaving one's home country is an act of deracination. The known is swapped for the unknown, the routine for the unusual—the familiar is made strange. The purpose of making-strange, as we know, is to awaken the senses and the mind. Exiles thus operate at a heightened level of attention upon their arrival. With their eyes wide open, they arrive into a space filled with the noise of culture, politics, and economy, and all that in a foreign language. Everything that is the resident hum of daily life for the natives makes for a sum of elements that need to be decoded by the exiles.

Information requires a clean and uniform background in order to function. (It is impossible to decode public address system announcements in a noisy environment or to read the words printed on a busy backdrop.) Exile makes the background crowded with tiny bits of information, with snippets of foreign language, new rules, different maps, conflicting longings. The noise permeates everyday life, thus making communication minimal or negligible. The information becomes coded and difficult to comprehend and use. In Lacanian terms, this effectively prevents the exile from reaching the mirror phase that is needed to enter the new society.

Performing exile thus means performing decryption.

Chris Abani, a Nigerian author who has been exiled both internally (when his father, a politician, renounced him) and externally (when he had to flee Nigeria after triple incarceration and a period on death row) claims,

> In a world that wants to control and classify its relationships with all individuals and groups, the exile is possibly the most frightening, because he or she occupies that liminal space that defies any category. This ideal "where" of exile, a physical, mental and imaginative place, as liminal as it is, has a concreteness to it, and I think all exiles would agree that one knows when one arrives there. This terra firma is however given its dimensions and shape by those not in exile. This liminal

space can be a wasteland often difficult to conceive—not only for the outsider, but for natives too—and so the process of rationalization begins: the construction of a consolation.

(Abani 24)

Željko G., a refugee from Sarajevo who had arrived with his family in Toronto in the early 1990s, performed the same task every morning in the first months after their arrival: he would take one of the buses that went from one end of the city to another and observe. The purpose of this exercise, he said, was to understand the city. With over two million citizens buttered over 1,800 square kilometres, Toronto was an over-compressed toponym, and Željko needed to cut it down to approachable bits. Measuring the size of the metropolis was only part of it; the more important segment of the process was to observe the change between the neighbourhoods—the architecture, the density of buildings, the frequency of strip malls, shopping centres, large crossroads connecting east and west, the increasing density towards the lake . . . Every day he would get out of the bus and take a little stroll through a different neighbourhood. Whilst doing this, he was listening to the sounds of tens of languages spoken in this truly multicultural hive. What Željko was doing was framing the city, both with a large frame of the overall crossword knowledge and with tens, nay, hundreds, of smaller local frames.

Frame is the border between chaos and organised space. By delineating a controlled space within the uncontrolled chaotic space, the *frame* becomes a central tool of decoding. The function of the frame is to focus the gaze on a certain image/idea/area/process. Framing parts of his new reality allowed Željko to perform the art every exile must master: the process of rationalisation thus beginning the construction of his own consolation. By placing the controlled, isolated zones within the polyphonic area of the uncontrolled space, he established his ownership of the city.

***

Returning to the case of my translated memoir for one last time: at some point, I finally understood that the process of exile was irreversible.

My translated book was written in a language that perhaps was not mine, but it was the current language of the place I had abandoned. It was written by an author who was not the one who had left his country.

Whilst travelling through Serbia to promote the book, I felt like a representative of myself, not my actual self. I was performing myself. I was who I was not. I noticed that the effect of recognition was not even important anymore. Those who visited my readings came mostly without knowing who I had been or was—they came for the love of books, not for me. If exile meant making-strange, and habituation in the new environment meant un-making-strange, going back to the native culture did not mean undoing this mess. It meant making-very-very-strange.

Works cited

Abani, Chris. "Resisting the Anomie: Exile and the Romantic Self." *Creativity in Exile*, edited by Michael Hanne, Rodopi, 2004, pp. 21–30.

Boym, Svetlana. "Estrangement as a Lifestyle: Shklovsky And Brodsky." *Exile and Creativity: Signposts, Travellers, Outsiders, Backward Glances*, edited by Susan Rubin Suleiman, Duke UP, 1998, pp. 241–263.

Forsyth, Mark. "The Language Rules We Know—But Don't Know We Know." *BBC*, 8 Sept. 2016, www.bbc.com/culture/story/20160908-the-language-rules-we-know-but-dont-know-we-know. Accessed 31 May 2018.

Lahiri, Jhumpa. "Why Do Writers Abandon their Native Language?" *The Economist*, 14 Mar. 2016, www.economist.com/prospero/2016/03/14/why-do-writers-abandon-their-native-language. Accessed 15 Oct. 2018.

Rushdie, Salman. *The Satanic Verses*. Random House Trade, 2008.

Shaffer, Peter. *Amadeus*. Penguin Books, 2007.

Shklovsky, Viktor. "Art as Technique." *University of Warwick*, warwick.ac.uk/fac/arts/english/currentstudents/undergraduate/modules/fulllist/first/en122/lecturelist-2015-16-2/shklovsky.pdf. Accessed 3 June 2018.

Todorovic, Dragan. *The Book of Revenge: A Blues for Yugoslavia*. Random House Canada, 2006.

———. "In My Language I Am Smart." *Radio play/aural essay/sound art*. www.dragantodorovic.com/projects/in_my_language_I_am_smart.mp3. Accessed 25 June 2018.

Whorf, Benjamin Lee. "The Relation of Habitual Thought and Behavior to Language." *Sociolinguistics*. Modern Linguistics Series, edited by N. Coupland and A. Jaworski, Palgrave, 1997, pp. 443–463.

Part I

On migration and self-translation

3   Playing and writing across languages and cultures

Ana Candida Carneiro

I have lived in a foreign language for almost 20 years. This means I have spent half of my life talking, writing, and thinking through a linguistic framework that didn't organically grow within me since my earliest childhood experiences but was intentionally and laboriously acquired in later years by means of exposure to new cultures and intense readings. The sense of displacement that comes from this almost alienated existence is hard to navigate. There is always a part of me that longs for a reconnection to that original source, as pure as it is—that *mother tongue*—that shaped my consciousness as it came to inhabit this world—first as a baby, then as a child, then as a teenager, then as an adult.

The process of acquiring a language has always fascinated me and perhaps for this reason I have tried to recreate it so many times by learning other languages. The big step, though, the step to "other worlds," happened when I was 21. By immigrating first to Italy, and later to the United States, I became a writer in a foreign language. By leaving my country, I was initiated into what discrimination means and to that overwhelming sense of powerlessness that comes when you don't conform to a specific identity or possess enough knowledge or money to make you feel safe. The hurt faced by immigrants is often associated with a condition of forced invisibility. The psychology of the displaced in many instances oscillates across opposite poles: the need for recognition, assimilation, or the acquisition of a status like that of regular citizens and the need for preserving a connection to our roots. This intimate conflict is exasperated by discriminatory policies and behaviours. Immigrants are necessary, and yet we are an undesirable element that forces individuals and communities to face the fact that the world is bigger than they had pictured before and that their acquired certainties are just what they should be: temporary and relative. Like mice in a room, we can stay as long as we "keep in our place" and do not disrupt the status quo. As long as we remain quiet, invisible, and odourless.

This idea has fuelled my debut as a playwright. My first play, *All Is Filthy in Wonderland*,[1] came about after my three years as an undocumented immigrant in Italy. I could not leave the country without the threat of being taken to a detention centre. The lack of documents provokes considerable trauma. My play takes place in a detention centre for undocumented immigrants, what was called a CPT, a Centre for Temporary Stay, back in 2009. These became a scandal in 2005 when the Italian journalist Fabrizio Gatti disguised himself as an undocumented immigrant and was confined at the infamous CPT of Lampedusa. No press had been given access to a CPT before. The result was a shocking document published by the magazine *L'Espresso*, denouncing all sorts of abuses. Men, women, and children were forced to live in calamitous, unhygienic conditions in overpopulated institutions, suffering from spreading disease and physical violence by the police. The journalist also denounced the total inadequacy of the expulsion procedure; after getting his "expulsion order," he was left in Agrigento to take whatever route he wanted.

My play tells the journey of two Brazilians sharing the same cell. Regina, who goes by the stage name "Jocasta," is a transgender performing artist who receives special favours from the director of the centre, such as having her own private cell, in exchange for sex. Sonia's arrival disrupts Regina's established routine. Regina initially repels the newcomer, perceiving her presence as an invasion of her space. She refuses to speak her native language, Portuguese—a psychological phenomenon observable in immigrant communities—whilst Sonia has very poor knowledge of Italian. Looking for some familiar ground, Sonia confronts Regina about her refusal to speak Portuguese and to acknowledge their common cultural heritage:

SONIA: Você fala Português. Você fala Português, eu ouvi. Você é brasileira.
[. . .]
REGINA: Let me put this straight. This cage is mine. You are just a guest. So
be a good girl or you are gonna be in trouble, understand?
SONIA (*to herself*): Roberto Carlos. Eu ouvi. No rádio.
Sonia takes the radio in her hands very carefully, as a precious object.
[. . .]
REGINA: Give it to me! It's MINE. MI-NE, understand? And don't you dare
touch my things again! (*Pushing Sonia*) Your place is there. See this
line? (*She draws with her hand or foot a line, indicating an unequal
division of the space*) You stay there. This part is all mine. Understand?
UN-DER-STAND?

(Carneiro 2014, unpublished manuscript 5)

The dynamic between Sonia and Regina reenacts the discrimination and exclusion that immigrants face on a social level by the native population.

Though an immigrant herself, Regina enjoys the power of having been longer in a place, having developed relationships that allow her to behave the way she does. The newcomer is perceived as a threat to her established order and acquired privileges, and she has to keep Sonia "in her place" by drawing a clear line between her wider territory and possessions in the cell. Sonia is often made invisible by Regina, who doesn't answer her questions and requests. Regina behaves like a true European (or Italian) by adopting her second language as if it were her first and impersonating Italian singers as an artistic choice. She takes the colonial mentality to its paroxysm by totally identifying with the dominant culture. Demoralised by this burdensome situation, Sonia starts to write letters to her family and lying about her conditions. Back in Brazil, her family thinks that she is now rich and well married. By creating an alternative identity and narrative for herself, Sonia gains some illusion of control over her own life. A kind of alliance slowly develops between the two inmates as Regina notices Sonia's fascination with her artistry. Somehow, art is what unites them and creates understanding—Sonia, the storyteller, and Regina-Jocasta, the performer—both trying to fulfil their dream of a better life, both alienated and crushed by a racist and bigoted society, both trying to become an "Other" to themselves. As the drama of institutional oppression unfolds, Sonia and Regina become as necessary as sunlight to each other.

It is actually the impulse to *internal otherness*, besides the social, external one, which constitutes the core of the drama of the displaced. To live in limbo is agonising, so immigrants, especially undocumented ones, often consciously or unconsciously lean towards becoming an Other within: one who belongs, one who is seen, one who has space. When the external world does not provide the conditions for the actualisation of this inner movement, immigrants are thrown into a loop that ignites processes of mental alienation. This explains the high level of psychiatric disorders in these populations. At the end of my play, in fact—after Regina's untreated tuberculosis leads to her death—Sonia swallows the sleeping pills that her friend had been accumulating.

All Is Filthy in Wonderland puts the immigrant's undesirable bodies at the centre of the stage. By exploring the theatricality of bilingualism—the play is written in Italian, but dialogues intertwine Italian and Portuguese and no translation or subtitles are made available during the performance—the audience is placed in a condition of "foreignness," unable to understand every word. I wanted to demand from those watching my play the same effort that migrants have to make to overcome linguistic barriers. In a foreign land where you don't speak the language well, your body and soul are consumed in an immense, constant effort of de-codification. You go into an energy-consuming state of heightened awareness. Dramaturgically speaking, whilst writing the play, I had to find the right balance in the use of the two languages so that the audience would understand enough to be engaged in the story but at the same time be denied a full understanding of the communication happening onstage. By demanding from the audience the same effort that immigrants have to make to understand their surroundings, I wanted to induce the audience to reach a new level of empathy: not just the relative empathy of watching a show from a distanced perspective, as if looking through a window into a world that belongs to an Other, but also the *radical empathy* of inhabiting and experiencing as a community the same space as the actors.

The question of the audience has always fascinated me. Plays are always a gesture towards someone, both on a social and a spiritual level. We are used to thinking about the audience as singular, but the writer, in the process of writing, is often negotiating with a myriad of different potential audiences that arise in their imagination. For this reason, a single play can have more than one *implied audience*. Similar to Iser's concept of "implied reader"—an architecture of "response giving structures" built by the author whilst writing the literary text—the "implied audience" corresponds to the expected effects that the playwright wants to produce as the play is staged (Iser 34). For a migrant writer, especially, there is a constant negotiation that contemplates an overlap of cultural and linguistic experiences and realities. Am I writing to Brazilian immigrants in Italy or to Italian audiences? Or both? How does this thought change the way I am writing? I think that all writers ultimately write for that spiritual audience within themselves, but we cannot ignore those other contextual audiences who are embedded in the situations in which we are submerged and in the impact we imagine for our work. When conceiving a project, it is necessary to come to terms with the theatre culture we are working in and the theatre professionals that surround us. For immigrant artists, this implies getting acquainted with a landscape of expectations that might be very different from those we are used to.

The question I often ask myself is can I imagine a generic abstract audience, which is not rooted in a particular culture? Especially when you start thinking globally and transculturally, this is a temptation. For now, my answer is no. A play written in Italian, whilst I am living in Italy, will necessarily be a different play than one written in English, whilst I am living in America, even if I am exploring the same topic, images, or ideas. For example, the writing process for my latest full-length play, *The Unfit*, started whilst I was still in Italy and concluded after I moved to America.[2] Because of this geographic and cultural transition, my imagination shifted, which affected the characters, structure, and dynamics of the play. In this particular work, still first written entirely in Italian, I used translation as a second creative step. The implication of including translation in the writing process adds a layer of complexity and awkwardly interesting linguistic and theatrical transformations. For example, a character first imagined as white suddenly became African American, giving the play a completely different set of meanings and leveraging the discourse about race that was already in it.

Migrant writers have a wider array of references constituting our own specific expandable and malleable artistic lens. This lens allows us to speak transnationally. Nevertheless, we cannot avoid the fact that we are influenced by our immediate environment or that we want to speak to the contexts we operate in. This is particularly true for playwrights because our work is usually only fully accomplished when it is staged. So there's always a gesture towards real, specific communities that will constitute real, specific audiences, as well as the need at least to acknowledge the aesthetic canons of specific producing realities.

All Is Filthy in Wonderland adopts a hyperrealist aesthetic with bursts of surreal moments. Exploring the thematic axes of clean/dirty, invisible/visible, inside/outside—immigrants are dirty, therefore, they must be secluded and removed from view, kept on the margins—the script also actively solicits the audience's sense of smell to create an immersive effect. For as much as a society would like to repel otherness and preserve a sense of control over its own territory and cultural constructs, the reality of global migratory movements cannot be avoided or denied. In the same way, the bad smell of the CPT's neglected latrines invades the whole theatre, reminding us that human beings are human beings, no more nor less, and they should not be treated like unwanted animals. The enveloping odour not only denounces the abuses in a particular social-historical situation but also reminds us of that uncomfortable zone of bias in each of us. For as much as we would like to believe that discrimination is a problem of the state, it is actually ourselves—or that part in ourselves that wants to preserve power over a circumstance by excluding, neglecting, or criticising those who are different and who because of their difference make us feel threatened—who perpetuate cycles of oppression and exclusion.

At the end of *All Is Filthy in Wonderland*, Sonia receives her *foglio di via*, her expulsion order. Funnily (or tragically) enough, years later, after I had acquired my citizenship through marriage, I also received my *foglio di via*. A Kafkaesque burp of bureaucracy—the process had come to its conclusion, even though I already enjoyed a new legal status. I have it with me, framed—to remind myself of a past that is still present. I found my voice as an artist through immigration, by existing in the condition of otherness, by making foreign languages my own. Had I not crossed the line and reached other worlds, my poetics and even my aesthetic choices would have been much narrower and unidimensional. My life as a writer would have been easier, for sure: I would have been more "classifiable," more visible, more acceptable, more convenient; I would have avoided many forms of discrimination. However, could I have lived with myself by not pursuing my dreams? I don't think so. Re-routing my existence more than once became my fertile ground, my own artistic way of inhabiting the world—and I'm very proud of it.

Notes

1 *All Is Filthy in Wonderland* was shortlisted for the Riccione Prize, the most important playwriting award in Italy. Nevertheless, as a testament to the fact that immigrants still have problems being accepted in their new cultures, it never received a professional production in Italy. It was staged in March 2009 at the Paolo Grassi Conservatory of Dramatic Arts, in Milan as part of my senior thesis in playwriting. Two non-professional actors, Margot Minelli and Wana Reis, who are Brazilian immigrants themselves, beautifully performed the role of Regina-Jocasta and Sonia.

2 I immigrated to the United States in 2015. I started to write *The Unfit* in 2013 and finished the play in 2017. *The Unfit* is a play about the perversions of the fertility and art industries in the age of global capitalism.

Works cited

Carneiro, Ana C. *All is Filthy in Wonderland*. Unpublished Manuscript, 2014.

———. "E' Tutto Sporco nel Paese delle Meraviglie." *Rivista Dramma*, 2014, www.dramma.it/dati/libreria/tuttosporco.htm. English translation by Letizia Olivieri, unpublished.

———. *The Unfit*. Unpublished Manuscript, 2017.

De Andrade, Oswald, and Leslie Bary. "Cannibalist Manifesto." *Latin American Literary Review*, vol. 19, no. 38, 1991, pp. 38–47.

Gatti, Fabrizio. "Io Clandestino a Lampedusa". *L'Espresso*, 7 Oct. 2005, http://espresso.repubblica.it/palazzo/2005/10/07/news/io-clandestino-a-lampedusa-1.594. Accessed 13 May 2019.

Iser, Wolfgang. *The Act of Reading: A Theory of Aesthetic Response*. Johns Hopkins UP, 1978.

4 Acting as the act of translation
Domesticating and foreignising strategies as part of the actor's performance in the Irish-Polish production of *Bubble Revolution*

Kasia Lech

This chapter considers how multilingual and transnational actors can facilitate and actively contribute to new ways of translating theatre and performing translation and, by doing so, open new dramaturgical avenues and promote theatre's engagement with mobility. The article's focus, however, is not how migration experience informs translation (Polezzi 346), but how translation strategies become creative tools for multilingual and transnational dramaturgy and its performance. In the current context, transnationalism indicates "the crossing of cultural, ideological, linguistic, and geopolitical borders and boundaries of all types but especially those of nation-states" (Duff 57). I argue that translation strategies empower actors to take control over their creative destiny, highlight their authorship of the theatre event, and shape their representation within transnational socio-political and cultural spaces, whilst also adding layers to the actors' characterisation techniques. This process allows the actor to further challenge linear ideas on the relationship between the source and translation (Marinetti 130; Polezzi 350), broaden the spaces of cultural representation and encounter, and engage with socio-political discourses by creating new dramaturgies of foreignness. It also brings a new perspective on the inseparability of performative and linguistic aspects of theatre translation, which Cristina Marinetti recently marked as a significant challenge for theatre scholarship (128–129). By arguing these points, the chapter pushes a popular translator-performer metaphor (e.g., Johnston; Espasa) beyond its figurative dimension. As the article explores how an actor can actively employ and embody translation, it also expands the previous arguments for the potential of transnational and multilingual actors to challenge homogeneous and stable identities and geographies (Nascimento 7, 136; McIvor 86, 105–106; Grossman 60, 79). *Active* is a keyword here, as it marks the translation strategies as means of expression that the actor can creatively and purposefully transform and use to facilitate the actor's creative aims, the production's dramaturgy, and larger socio-cultural dialogues.

The example under discussion is the Irish-Polish staging of a one-woman play about growing up in Poland in the 1980s: *Rewolucja Balonowa* (*Bubble Revolution*) by Julia Holewińska.[1] Artur Zapałowski translated and John Currivan directed the play for Polish Theatre Ireland. The focus is the creative process I employed as a Polish-born and -trained actor co-creating and performing the production whilst living variously in Poland, Ireland, and the United Kingdom. *Bubble Revolution* (Figure 4.1), since its Dublin premiere in 2013, has been performed approximately 50 times in Ireland and the United Kingdom. In particular, I focus on the 2016 Edinburgh Fringe Festival as part of my practice-as-research project that started after the 2013 Dublin run. The initial process already involved cultural and linguistic translations, reflecting the idea of collaborative translation as a "microcosm" in which "landscapes of reception are inhabited, shaped, and negotiated by different producers" (Marinetti and Rose 173). For example, as the mise-en-scène facilitated performances in Polish and in English, I needed to engage during English-language performances in "live" interpreting of three popular Polish songs that Holewińska wrote into the play. Currivan and I changed Zapałowski's translations of the songs so they fitted with the rhythm and tempo of the music and so I could sing an English-language translation over Polish-language recordings. My subsequent practice-as-research project was inspired by Helen Cusack's review in which she commented on issues of intelligibility related to my accent and cultural references in the text. Whilst she praised my "skilled and charismatic" performance, she also noted that my "accent is difficult to understand," and because of that, "many names and cultural references are unfortunately lost" (Cusack). In response, I asked how I could use my "foreignness" (including my accent) to facilitate audience engagement with the translation of Holewińska's play.

In my creative process, I explored Lawrence Venuti's two extreme types of translation strategies: "domestication" and "foreignisation". The former, through its fluency of language, vocabulary, and ideas familiar to the target audience, makes for a comfortable encounter between the audience and the translated text. But Venuti champions the latter, which "resists dominant values in the receiving culture so as to signify the linguistic and cultural difference of the foreign text" and disrupts the expectations of the target cultural and linguistic contexts. Foreignising translation does not abandon fluency but "reinvents" it to "create new conditions of readability" (Venuti, *Invisibility* 12–19). In so doing, it can "promote cultural innovation as well as the understanding of cultural difference" and "precipitate social change" (Venuti, *Scandals* 11, 79).

Venuti also argues for the potential of translation to construct images and new "positions of intelligibility" of foreignness for the target audience (*Invisibility* 20). In other words, translation can have an impact on one's

Figure 4.1 *Bubble Revolution*; written by Julia Holewińska; Kasia Lech as Vica with
picture of Russian hypnotherapist Anatoly Mikhailovich Kashpirovsky.
September 2013. Theatre Upstairs. Dublin

Credit: Photo by Polish Theatre Ireland/Silver Merick Studio

perception of a foreign culture, on how one interacts with that culture, and
how one's perception of oneself is changed through that foreign culture and
in position to that foreign culture. By turning Venuti's concepts into acting tools, I aimed at facilitating the intelligibility of Holewińska's text by
having the audience recognise themselves in the foreignness of the play—
rather than by identifying domestic values inscribed within it—and in turn
find new ways to engage with foreignness. The upcoming discussion looks
at *Bubble Revolution* as the act of multi-layered translation that is both linguistic and contextual, both textual and performative, and both domesticat-
ing and foreignising. I discuss strategies used to incorporate translation into
my performance of the character Wiktoria (who is transformed into Vica
later in the text) and of *Bubble Revolution* as a manifesto of foreignness
which links with aspects of translation featuring in Holewińska's play and
with the play as a generational manifesto.

Rewolucja Balonowa is Wiktoria's monologue in response to her 5-year-
old son Janek's request for a fairy tale. Whilst Wiktoria does not direct her

own coming-of-age story at Janek, she is "rehearsing" it for a person who does not share these memories, and she explains some peculiarities of life in Poland in the 1980s and 1990s (see Figure 4.3). Her first experiences of tasting Coca-Cola overlap with Polish society in the aftermath of martial law, struggling with the reality of rationed food and queues. Poland defeats communism and steps into the world of democracy and capitalism as Vica's hair starts growing under her arms (see Figure 4.2), and she discovers the taste of cheap wine and bad sex. Poland's entry into the European Union (EU) opens the gate for Vica's romance with an unnamed and married Italian man. As the play progresses, Vica translates her name from Wiktoria to Vica (its anglicised version). In Venuti's terms (*Invisibility* 20), her perception of her identity changes in response to Western—and predominantly American— culture. As Vica tries to fit her history into the conventions of fairy tales, the text reveals that Vica manipulates that history. Her fairy tale is, in fact, a story of loneliness: freedom and capitalism brought her disappointment, anxiety, and depression. Vica wants to start another revolution but she sees nothing left to fight for. The play leaves her struggling with identity.

Rewolucja Balonowa reflects the experiences of "generation nothing," those Poles born in the 1980s who were the first Polish generation for a very long time that had no generational fight or collective social aim (Wandacho-wicz). Although today's political crises in Poland may have changed that for some, the lack of a revolutionary cause is at the heart of Holewińska's play. As a result, says Joanna Derkaczew, *Rewolucja* presents the Poles born in the 1980s as completely immobilised by their powerful collective bond of "shame, disappointment, and pain of being abandoned" (my translation). "Generation nothing" also comprises the majority of those who emigrated from Poland to the United Kingdom and Ireland after Poland joined the EU in May 2004 (Okólski and Salt 18; Krings et al. 41). In this context, Derkaczew's point gets another layer. Vica's "immobilisation" is highlighted when she expresses her simultaneous need and inability to find a revolutionary cause just as she talks about different stereotypes of Polish people in the West: "Car-thieves, drunks, trouble-makers" (Holewińska, *Bubble Revolution* 24). Ironically, these and other stereotypes are precisely the fight that many Poles are facing in their everyday lives as "foreigners", which was particularly prominent during my rehearsals for the Fringe 2016 as the United Kingdom was debating Brexit.[2] This became a meeting point between the source text and my application of translation strategies.

As the spectator's goodwill plays a key part in a multilingual production's ability to communicate with its audiences (Carlson 53), a key idea underlying my approach was what Lindsay B. Cummings describes as a "dialogic empa-thy": an emotional connection based on a "constant and open-ended engage-ment" between the actor and the audience. Such a definition does not assume

Figure 4.2 Bubble Revolution; written by Julia Holewińska; Kasia Lech as Vica
during Vica's first visit in a Western supermarket. September 2013.
Theatre Upstairs. Dublin

Credit: Photo by Polish Theatre Ireland/Silver Merick Studio

any simplistic identification, but instead it appears through the spectators'
and actor's mutual recognition of and responses to each other (Cummings
4–6). This is important for *Bubble Revolution* as a manifesto of identity that
is constantly renegotiated through the recognition of and responses between
itself and other cultures it encounters. Cummings also echoes my own
approach to theatre translation as a process of constant "cultural re-evaluation"
(Johnston, 27) and Homi Bhabha's description of performing "foreignness"
as difference through a process of connection that is "a complex, on-going
negotiation that seeks to authorize cultural hybridities" (2).

I facilitate the translational potential of "dialogic empathy", even before
the performances start. In Canterbury (2014), for example, there was an
interactive exhibition that offered spectators an opportunity to experience
some cultural references from the play, finding points of connection to the
foreign reality presented, and thus to me as the character and me as a "foreigner".[3] For the Fringe performances, because of the nature of the festival,
this exhibition was transformed into a virtual one (Lech, *Bubble Revolution*), and I also welcomed each spectator by offering cards with selected

memories and some sensory experiences of communist queues, as well as sweets.[4] In live performances, I embody translation strategies to allow the audience to find their points of connection to the story and my foreignness. As Vica and I renegotiate our identity (and the text of the translation) in response to the cultural contexts we have encountered (partly through the audience), spectators may open themselves to a similar process. By facilitating the spectators' search for new ways to respond to my foreignness, I work to strengthen the political potential arising from the translational context.

I start the English-language play in Polish: "Wszystko zaczęło się od gumy do żucia" (Holewińska, *Rewolucja* 1), which I immediately translate: "It all started with bubble gum" (Holewińska, *Bubble Revolution* 1). The Polish line is a spontaneous reaction to discovering childhood treasures; the English one recognises the presence of the audience and that they might not have understood what I said. I set myself an action[5] "to translate" and, by doing so, highlight differences between contexts of the source and the translation. It also immediately puts me-as-Vica in the role of a translator, which I sustain throughout the play. For example, when Vica has a phone conversation in Polish, I explain it in English. She also finds an echoing of her affair with an Italian man in a Polish anthem that features the line "Z ziemi włoskiej do Polski" (Holewińska, *Rewolucja* 4), "To Poland from the Italian land." I sing it in Polish and translate it into English.

I also provide a "footnote" (italicised in the following examples) to selected cultural references. For instance, at the start of the play, Vica tells her father's fairy tale about Lenin who "farted all the time". She explains that only at home could her father "be so coarsely visceral" (Holewińska, *Bubble Revolution* 3). Vica does not explain the reasons as they were part of the historical context of Poland in the early 1980s.[6] Because at first spectators did not understand the joke, I now say, "But *with the General, Martial Law, and communist police everywhere*, it was only at home that he allowed himself to be so coarsely visceral" (Holewińska, *Bubble Revolution* 3). Another "footnote" has to do with money, so I translate Polish złoty to British pounds. Vica now says, "[He] pays 400 złoty—*80 pounds*—a month in child support" (Holewińska, *Bubble Revolution* 5).

In Dublin English-language performances, I sang an English-language translation over Polish-language recordings, so the audience understood the text. Now, my "live interpreting" of the songs is also linked with Vica's story. As a case in point, Vica talks about unpaid bills and something she is not ready for—the need to take responsibility for herself; this is accompanied by a phone ringing, which she is afraid to answer, scared of her obligations. A song *Telefony* by Republika is the focus point here: I sing it in both Polish and English to illustrate Vica's struggles. The final stanza sounds like this:

> telefony w mojej głowie (in my head the phone is ringing)
> in my head the phone is ringing
> in my head w mojej głowie (in my head)
> it's only me!
>
> (Holewińska, *Bubble Revolution* 9)

I direct English lines at the audience, and I position myself close to them. I sing the Polish text without any eye contact and from the upstage corners. Vica's action in English is "to calm everyone down"; in Polish it is "to hide". I add another link between Vica's story and the act of translation as she comments on the drab monochrome of capitalism, where "everything everywhere" is the same (Holewińska, *Bubble Revolution* 23). This line is repeated several times: a mixture of Polish and English that compete with each other. This tension between the source and the translation is meant to add more layers to Vica's struggles and illustrate that Vica's story is a complex translation both in language and in meaning. To use Eva Espasa's metaphor of translator as performer (40–41), this type of translation can mask Vica's experiences. It can also present her as a dramaturg: someone who can control and manipulate the narrative. This action is in line with Vica's attempts to "translate" her history into a fairy tale and hide her anxiety. Vica-dramaturg also attempts to take ownership of her story and its staging.

I explore this metaphor further by disrupting the fluency of Zapałowski's translation and claiming my ownership of English as a non-native speaker. I challenge those mono- and ethnolinguistic perspectives that set the English of the Anglo-Saxon world as the norm from which other forms of English derive or which they abuse (Kachru and Nelson 14–21). In doing so, I go beyond the simple fact of my accent and beyond my characterisation and engage with the issue on a dramaturgical level to highlight the presence of a foreign individual and the foreign origin of the text. My focus is on responding to the transnational context of *Bubble Revolution* and accounting for different situations and inputs like media, travelling, popular culture, or schools in which one learns to speak English as a foreign language (Kachru and Nelson 18).

Zapałowski translated the play with many Americanisations. For instance, his Vica curses using "goddamn" and comments on her school experience referring to the American system of education, such as first grade, fifth grade, and so on. Zapałowski's choices fit well with Vica's fascination with the United States and the West in general; they also highlight Vica's attempts to "translate" herself into Western culture. However, I wanted to highlight Vica's identity, as well as the translated play and the production, as a complex transnational hybrid that refuses any fixed or monochrome representation. This echoes Vica's comment that monochrome reality replaced her colourful dreams.

With the help of Janet Morgan, I introduced Dublin influences into my speech; my Irish accent becomes more audible when Vica's emotions rise and when she has less control over her public self. Vica is trying to "correct" her Irish sounds with failed attempts at standard British pronunciation. She complains about her life saying, "Our bloody Polish bad luck" (Holewińska, *Bubble Revolution* 5); I pronounce "bloody" and "luck" with the Dublin Irish [ʊ] instead of /ʌ/, whilst at the same time stating that Vica and I are Polish. Another word I play on is "bubble", pronounced whenever Vica feels in control as [bʌbl] and, in moments when Vica's mask starts stripping off, as [bʊbl]. To take it further, English-language posters inform the audience that the play is "performed in English with a Polish accent and a slight touch of Irish". All this highlights numerous tensions between the source context and its translation. Playing with various kinds of English allows me to reflect on the shifts within today's migration and linguistic soundscapes of the British Isles, traditionally shaped by Britain's colonial past. Poles are now the largest foreign-born community in the United Kingdom and Ireland (White; Ireland, *Census* 50), and many Poles move between Ireland and the United Kingdom, as the British and Irish themselves have done for centuries. Today, when the Polish language is heard adopting multiple languages, accents, and dialects across the British Isles, Seamus Heaney's famous point that language is "one of the places we all live" (277) gains new relevance.

Moreover, translation helps me further facilitate "dialogic empathy" (Cummings 4–6). An example includes teaching spectators a Polish word: "Babcia" (Granny). When Vica talks about her grandmother, I use the word "Babcia" but translate it only the first two times. By making "Babcia" the only Polish word that Vica shares with her audience, I mark Vica's relationship with this person and this word as special. This gesture implies that Vica trusts the audience enough to share the word "Babcia". This becomes even more apparent when Vica recalls her grandmother's dying of cancer because the hospital queue is too long. This is likely to resonate with experiences of the National Health Service crisis in the United Kingdom.

My continuous attention to the presence of the audience adds emphasis to my live presence as a performer. Because the play is in the first person, with Vica also "performing" her story, and because Vica and I are the same age and from the same place, my identity as an actor and as a character overlap. The context of translation both intensifies and adds additional layers to this overlap. Both as Vica and as an actor, I express myself in a language that is not my

Figure 4.3 Bubble Revolution; written by Julia Holewińska; Kasia Lech as Vica recalls her journey from Poland to Sweden in a Polonez car. September 2013. Theatre Upstairs. Dublin

Credit: Photo by Polish Theatre Ireland/Silver Merick Studio

own; consequently, my status as a translator encompasses my identities as an actor and as a character, which complicates the visibility and invisibility of the translation and the relationship between foreign and target contexts. Such an overlap, as Bert O. States argues (119), can enable the audience to engage emotionally both with Vica and with me as a performer.[7] As the foreignising elements of translation remind the audience of my status as a foreigner, they also highlight an increased risk of a mistake, which, as States notes, can highlight my vulnerability as a performer and evoke spectators' empathy (States 119). This "dialogic empathy" further strengthens the political potential of *Bubble Revolution* by generating an impact on how one relates to and interacts with a Polish person and culture and how one's perception of oneself is changed through Polishness and in position to Polishness (Venuti, *Invisibility* 20). As Latimer states in his review, the piece "contemplates how Britain and the U.S. are the very countries that drive the mass movement of people, yet then demonise those same individuals in the process" (2016).

"Translation wields enormous power in constructing representations of foreign cultures", says Venuti (*Scandals* 67). In *Bubble Revolution*, the ownership of this representation is taken back by the source culture rather than the target one. By revealing Vica's status as a translator and dramaturg of her own story and by highlighting the live presence of the foreign individual translating it for the audience, the production confronts the audience with a foreign actor. This foreign individual escapes a stable, one-dimensional identity and claims co-ownership over her representation on the English-language stages and over broader dramaturgies of foreignness. *Bubble Revolution* showcases how translation empowers the actor, and it points towards the still unexplored potential of both non-native English accents onstage and of actors "performing" translations. As the play is a manifesto of a generation that struggles with identity, the translation adds another dramaturgical dimension to the play. In this sense, *Bubble Revolution* offers another example of how translation enriches the source text and offers additional layers of meaning rather than compromising the source's integrity.

Notes

1 *Rewolucja Balonowa* in this chapter always refers to the source text in Polish; *Bubble Revolution* indicates its English-language version.
2 The debate represented Polish people in stereotypical roles like plumber, criminal, or a benefit taker, often threatening native structures – e.g., Anushka Asthana. "Vote Leave Releases List of Serious Crimes by EU Citizens in Britain." *The Guardian*, 29 Mar. 2016, www.theguardian.com/politics/2016/mar/28/vote-leave-releases-list-of-serious-crimes-by-eu-citizens-in-britain; Paola Buonadonna. "First They Came for the Polish Plumbers: a Dystopian view of Life Post-Brexit." *Telegraph*, 3 June 2016, www.telegraph.co.uk/news/2016/06/03/first-they-came-for-the-polish-plumbers-a-dystopian-view-of-life/; and Rebecca Perring. "How to Get 'GENEROUS' British Benefits: Shocking Guide Handed out to Polish Migrants." *Express*, 10 Mar. 2016, www.express.co.uk/news/uk/651386/Polish-migrant-guide-British-benefits-system-welfare-hand-outs-unemployed.
3 For a video recording of the exhibition, see Jamie Mepham. "*Bubble Revolution*: Journey back to 1980s and 1990s Poland." *Bubble Revolution*, 16 May 2016, bubblerevolution.com/?p=766.
4 For a discussion on memories in *Bubble Revolution*, see Kasia Lech, "Claiming Their Voice: Foreign Memories on the Post-Brexit British Stage." *Migration/Representation/Stereotypes*, edited by Yana Meerzon et al., Palgrave, 2020.
5 I use the term "actioning" to refer to an acting technique of scoring each thought in the text with a single action based on a transitive verb.
6 For more see Norman Davis. *Heart of Europe: The Past in Poland's Present.* Oxford UP, 2001, pp. 9–55.
7 This was documented by several reviewers (e.g., Awde; Hall).

Works cited

Awde, Nick. "*Bubble Revolution* Review at New Town Theatre, Edinburgh— 'Essential Viewing'." *The Stage*, 26 Aug. 2016, www.thestage.co.uk/reviews/2016/bubble-revolution-review-at-new-town-theatre-edinburgh-essential-viewing/.

Bhabha, Homi K. *The Location of Culture*. Routledge, 1994.

Carlson, Marvin. *Speaking in Tongues*. U of Michigan P, 2006.

Cummings, Lindsay B. *Empathy as Dialogue in Theatre and Performance*. Palgrave, 2016.

Cusack, Helen. "Bubble Revolution." *Irish Theatre Magazine*, 12 Sep. 2013, itmarchive.ie/web/Reviews/Current/Bubble-Revolution.aspx.html.

Derkaczew, Joanna. "Hit: *Rewolucja balonowa*" (Hit: *Bubble Revolution*). *Wysokie Obcasy*, 15 Dec. 2012, www.wysokieobcasy.pl/wysokie-obcasy/1,96856,10784 628,Hit__Rewolucja_balonowa__kit__Osadzeni__Mlynska.html.

Duff, Patricia A. "Transnationalism, Multilingualism, and Identity." *Annual Review of Applied Linguistics*, vol. 35, 2015, pp. 57–80.

Espasa, Eva. "Masks, Music Scores and Hourglasses: Rethinking Performability Through Metaphors." *Theatre Translation in Performance*, edited by Silvia Bigliazzi et al., Routledge, 2013, pp. 38–49.

Grossman, Elwira M. "Dwu(wielo)języczny teatr w zglobalizowanym kontekście brytyjskim, czyli o różnych stylach dramatu migracyjno-transkulturowego." *Teksty Drugie*, no. 3, 2016, pp. 60–80.

Hall, Ian D. "Bubble Revolution." *Liverpool Sound and Vision Rating*, 13 Aug. 2016, www.liverpoolsoundandvision.co.uk/2016/08/13/bubble-revolution-theatre-review-new-town-theatre-edinburgh-fringe-festival-2016/.

Heaney, Seamus. "Frontiers of Writing." *The Redress of Poetry*. Faber & Faber, 2011, pp. 256–293.

Holewińska, Julia. "Bubble Revolution." Translated by Artur Zapałowski with edits and changes by Kasia Lech and John Currivan, 2013. Theatrical script.

———. "Rewolucja Balonowa." 2011. Theatrical script.

Ireland. "Census 2016 Summary Results—Part 1." *Central Statistics Office*, 2017.

Johnston, David. "Metaphor and Metonmy: The Translator-Practitioner's Visibility." *Staging and Performing Translation: Text and Theatre Practice*, edited by Roger Baines et al., Palgrave, 2011, pp. 11–30.

Kachru, Braj B., and Cecil L. Nelson. "World Englishes." *Analysing English in a Global Context. A Reader*, edited by Anne Burns and Caroline Coffin, Routledge, 2001, pp. 9–25.

Krings, Torben, et al. *New Mobilities in Europe: Polish Migration to Ireland Post-2004*. Manchester UP, 2016.

Latimer, Andrew. "Bubble Revolution." *Fest*, 12 Aug. 2016, www.festmag.co.uk/theatre/103413-bubble-revolution.

Lech, Kasia. "Audience Reviews." *Bubble Revolution*, June 2016, bubblerevolution. com/?p=751.

———. *Bubble Revolution*, June 2016, bubblerevolution.com.

Marinetti, Cristina. "Theatre as a 'Translation Zone': Multilingualism, Identity and the Performing Body in the Work of Teatro delle Albe." *The Translator*, 2018, pp. 128–146.

Marinetti, Cristina, and Margaret Rose. "Process, Practice and Landscapes of Reception: An Ethnographic Study of Theatre Translation." *Translation Studies*, vol. 6, no. 2, 2013, pp. 166–182.

McIvor, Charlotte. *Migration and Performance in Contemporary Ireland Towards a New Interculturalism*. Palgrave, 2016.

50   *Kasia Lech*

Nascimento, Cláudia Tatinge. *Crossing Cultural Borders Through the Actor's Work: Foreign Bodies of Knowledge.* Routledge, 2009.

Okólski, Marek, and John Salt. "Polish Emigration to the UK after 2004, Why Did So Many Come?" *Central and Eastern European Migration Review,* vol. 3, no. 2, 2014, pp. 11–37.

Polezzi, Loredana. "Translation and Migration." *Translation Studies,* vol. 5, no. 3, 2012, pp. 345–356.

States, Bert O. *Great Reckonings in Little Rooms: On the Phenomenology of Theater.* U of California P, 1985.

Venuti, Lawrence. *The Scandals of Translation: Towards an Ethics of Difference.* Routledge, 1998.

———. *The Translator's Invisibility: A History of Translation.* Routledge, 2008.

Wandachowicz, Kuba. "Generacja Nic". *Gazeta Wyborcza,* 5 Sept. 2002, wyborcza. pl/1,75410,10939975,Generacja_Nic.html.

White, Nicola. "Population of the U.K. by Country of Birth and Nationality: 2015." *Office for National Statistics,* 25 Aug. 2016, www.ons.gov.uk/peoplepopulation andcommunity/populationandmigration/internationalmigration/bulletins/uk populationbycountryofbirthandnationality/august2016.

5 Heteroglossia in theatre of engagement

The case of *Khasakkinte Ithihasam*

Ameet Parameswaran

The problematics of migration in the field of theatre practices in India is often framed within the rubric of two related concerns: the debates around the practice and theorisations of intercultural theatre and the concept of hybridity as theorised within the postcolonial framework (Bhabha 1994; Bharucha 1997; Kapur 1997). The primary entry point for interculturalism in relation to India has been the theatrical practices of the late twentieth century. Theatre scholarship has problematised the "universalism" underlying theatre practices that claim to bring together cultures across national borders without recognising the economic and cultural base of power and hierarchy in the context of cultural imperialism (Bharucha 31–38). Against the universalising tendencies of interculturalism, Rustom Bharucha offered the term "intracultural", highlighting the need to foreground what can be seen as the problematics of internal migration and referring to "those exchanges within, between, and across regions in the larger framework of a nation" (31). He argued that "in our search for 'other cultures' we often forget the cultures within our own boundaries, the differences which are marginalized and occasionally silenced in our imagined homogeneities" (31). By foregrounding conflict and differentiation within territorial boundaries, Bharucha critiqued assimilationist tendencies to suggest that "before differences can be dissolved, they need to be acknowledged" (31).

With respect to hybridity, scholars have also foregrounded the space of the nation, especially the post-independent nation-states, in a more complex and nuanced manner in which the nation is construed as a site of conflictual and non-homogenous space yet offering a possibility of resistance to global capitalism (Cheah 157–197; Kapur 21–38; Bharucha 31–38). Specifically, scholars have critiqued the valorisation in Homi Bhabha's works of the unspecified categories of mobility and exile, as articulating a perspective of "metropolitan migrancy" (Cheah 157–197) or as an already arrived utopian metropolitan cosmopolitanism (Kapur 21–38), without taking into consideration the socio-political economy of multiple kinds of exiles. These theoretical concerns of interculturalism and hybridity have often been brought together and critically deployed in a self-reflexive manner in more recent works and as Una Chaudhuri points out "interculturalism is unravelling into, and re-forming out of, contemporary cultural theory, with results that promise to take theatre theory itself into an exciting new syncretic phase" (35). In this vein, for instance, intraculturalism has been used as a critical entry point to understand selfhood in exile (Meerzon 2009). Likewise, cross-cultural inter-action has been nuanced in a framework of cosmopolitanism wherein Gilbert and Lo, drawing on Hannerz's "description of cosmopolitanism as 'an intel-lectual and esthetic openness toward divergent cultural experiences,'" posit a "*cosmopolitics* that is caught up in hybrid spaces, entangled histories and complex human corporeographies" (11).

The present chapter interrogates how new dramaturgical techniques stages the encounter of a multiplicity of cultures to offer a new geogra-phy that is based on the effect of migration practices in the contemporary moment of globalisation. In a space such as India, wherein the nation-state itself recognizes the nation as a coming together of cultures through distinct state-recognised linguistic regions, can the multiplicity of languages and conflictual cultures that Bharucha points to be folded onto each other? If not, and one indeed registers a multiplicity of cultures and languages within what is otherwise deemed a single-language region, how do the languages of the stage embody the complexity of the contemporary experience of space and time? The present paper uses Marvin Carlson's theoretical focus on heteroglossia. Carlson argues that one needs to approach language as a "social construction, and that languages on the stage as elsewhere are rec-ognized and coded as languages by their employment of features culturally related to that construction rather than comprehension or noncomprehen-sion" (29). Carlson moves away from simply folding culture to language as he works through James Clifford's broader perspective to conceptualise stage language as involving cultures: "With expanded communication and intercultural influence, people interpret others, and themselves, in a bewil-dering diversity of idioms—a global condition of what Mikhail Bakhtin called 'heteroglossia'" (5). Carlson argues,

> In citing this usage, Clifford quotes Bakhtin's comment that hetero-glossia assumes that "languages do not *exclude* each other, but rather intersect with each other in many different ways," adding that 'what is said of languages applies equally to "cultures" and "subcultures".
>
> (5)

This chapter explores the complex intersection of languages in stage language by analysing the theatrical adaptation of O. V. Vijayan's iconic

Malayalam novel (1969), *Khasakkinte Ithihasam* (The Legends of Khasak, 2015; henceforward *Ithihasam*). The play was directed by Deepan Sivaraman with the group K. M. K. Smaraka Kalasamithi, which is based in the small town of Trikaripur in the south Indian state of Kerala. I interrogate the complex stage language of the production as an instance of what Andy Lavender has termed the "theatre of engagement," showing how a new heteroglossic language of the stage opens out a geography of contemporary experience based on migration in India under globalisation.

Ithihasam as theatre of engagement

The iconic novel *Ithihasam*, often regarded as the "'novel of the century' written in the Malayalam language" (Mukundan 86–87), is credited with the transformation of the Malayalam literary language itself. The novel constructs the village of Khasak, modelled on the village of Tasarak in Palaghat, North Kerala, as "a kind of nowhere land" (Raveendran 180) in the context of the newly independent Indian nation following its Nehruvian developmentalist path. The novel opens with the protagonist Ravi arriving in the village of Khasak to take charge as the sole teacher at the recently commissioned school. An excellent student of astrophysics, Ravi had been offered a fellowship at Princeton University but in existential angst has dropped out. Using the trope of Ravi's journey and encounter with the fantasy village of Khasak as an outsider, the novel presents the world of Khasak using a nonlinear narrative. As the writer M. Mukundan points out, this broke away from the socialist realism that had enjoyed a powerful hold on Malayalam literature until then. Mukundan highlights that in *Ithihasam*

> stark realism permeates the village, the characters and the language. But beneath the realism lies the magic of imageries. It's about life in the countryside, with realistic characters, with an over-arching rainbow of spirituality, punctuated by ceaseless self-interrogations. In the last analysis, it's the story of a distant village mired in local myths and legends, gathered in an urban gaze.
>
> (87)

The novel thereby opens up a new geography of the nation, foregrounding its polyphony of languages, beliefs, ritualistic practices, and superstitions, especially in the practices of two communities in Kerala, the Ezhavas (lower-caste Hindus) and the Rowthers (a Muslim community).

With an ensemble of more than 30 people, the theatrical adaptation can be seen as part of an emergent tendency in Indian theatre to move away from conventional norms. These performances often use new spaces and foreground sensory experience using fire, water, and earth onstage along-side live music and video projections. The three-hour, open-air performance of *Ithihasam*, for instance, was originally performed in Trikkaripur against the backdrop of a peepal tree with seats erected for audience on three sides and the centre space consisting of mud.[1] It stages divergent ritualistic prac-tices presented in the novel, such as oracles and preachers, using varied Islamic prayers and chanting, including the *bang vili* (prayer call) and non-mainstream but popular practices, such as rituals to drive djinns away or the ritual-healing performance of Teyyam from North Kerala. It also uses pup-petry, pre-recorded video projections of animations, and footage of alter-nate scapes of interaction between the characters in the performance and abstract images.

The aesthetic of *Ithihasam*, even as it works with a novel that sets out a space foregrounding diverse cultural practices outside the urban geography in India, presents a radical move away from what is theorised as the "the-atre of the roots" in the post-independence period. Drawing on the concept of hybridity from Homi Bhabha and putting forward the binary of Indian and the colonial, the theatre scholar Erin B. Mee, for instance, frames the theatre of the roots as a complex project that involves a "deliberate failure to decolonize" (130). In her close analysis of the practice of the signifi-cant director K. N. Panikkar from Kerala, Mee develops her formulation by reading Panikkar's performances as distinct from naturalism and indigenous performance. Mee highlights Panikkar's work as primarily a "performance driven theatre" (3) in which one can see a conscious move away from both play text and the centrality of plot as she argues that Panikkar's aesthetics lays stress on "multiple meanings" opened out by the performances through varied elaborations of a theme, where the question of "how" something happens is more critical than the "what" that happens. Mee highlights the "non-linguistic" aspect of performance in Panikkar's works, especially the use of body movement derived from *kalaripayattu*, rhythms, percussion, and music for communication of emotion. She argues that these practices use the proscenium stage; they position themselves away from and against both naturalism and indigenous performances. They produce a "deliberate failure" to "decolonize" fully, thereby challenging and redefining "Western notions of cultural modernity" (130).

The aesthetics of *Ithihasam*, on the other hand, without foregrounding the binary of the colonial and the Indian, posits a globality of contemporary experience in a space such as Kerala, an experience that need to be seen in light of what Hans-Thies Lehmann has famously termed "postdramatic the-atre". Lehmann focuses on the change in the conventional hierarchical rela-tion between text and theatrical sign in contemporary performances, arguing that "the step to postdramatic theatre is taken only when the theatrical means beyond language are positioned equally alongside the text and are systematically thinkable without it" (55). He argues that the "rupture" in postdramatic theatre, unlike earlier interventions, is that it does not cling "to the presentation of a fictive and simulated text-cosmos as a dominant" (55). Foregrounding the centrality of musicalisation and visualisation in performance, he further highlights that "within the paratactical, de-hierarchized use of signs postdramatic theatre establishes the possibility of dissolving the logocentric hierarchy and assigning the dominant role to elements other than dramatic logos and language" (93).

The beginning of the *Ithihasam* itself sets out the frame for an experience wherein theatrical means beyond language are highlighted. Unlike the novel that starts with the protagonist getting off the bus at the village of Khasak, the performance starts with setting up the mythological genealogy of Khasak narrated much later in the novel. As the performance begins, one sees burning torches in the darkness held by 30 figures spread behind the platform and the peepal tree. They slowly start moving upstage centre as a group, swaying the burning torches to the music of the distant lands with horse-trot rhythms and a narration begins:

> A long time ago, a long time ago, an army of 1001 horses came to Khasak. Sayyid Miyan Sheikh and his holy warriors. All horses were white, and strong. Except one. Sayyid Miyan Sheikh rode that old, weak grey horse. When that horse was tired, he ordered the army to stop. At the last hour of the night, the grey horse died.
>
> (*Ithihasam* 00:00:00–00:00:58)

The figures have reached the centre back and stand with raised burning torches. The narration continues: "He was laid to rest in Khasak's palm groves. Warriors decided to camp where the horse was buried. From that army was born the people of Khasak" (*Ithihasam* 00:01:03–00:01:15). The figures move slowly forward, swaying the burning torches as the rhythmic music merges with sounds of *bang vili* (Muslim prayer call).The performance ends in a similar way, with the choral composition performed by the whole cast.

Reviewers have noted this opening of the performance as a critical reinterpretation of the novel. K. P. Jayakumar highlights the scene and argues that through the appearance of the spirits of people who have died, *Ithihasam* "constructs an illusory world or parallel world of self-expression". He argues that they are "people who tell their biography from the end of what was said, from the end of what was seen, beyond this world, from the netherworld" (Jayakumar). What is being highlighted can be also be seen in a formal theatrical sense as the displacement of plot structure in postdramatic theatre as theorised by Lehmann where the present in postdramatic theatre is registered as appearance: "The present . . . [is] of a floating, fading presence—which at the same time enters experience as 'gone' (*fort*), as an absence, as an 'already leaving'—[and] crosses out dramatic representation" (144).

Whilst I will point to the particularity of the narratorial voice that restages the novel's language in the next section, here I will restrict myself to the overall approach of the adaptation to the world of Khasak. Whilst that world seems to emerge in appearance, unlike Lehmann's perspective, in fact, it is still very significant in the adaptation. For instance, Ragesh in his review highlights that rather than approaching the place through the perspective of the protagonist Ravi "who has left behind home, father and his beloved" to come to Khasak, the performance sidelines Ravi and foregrounds the place, Khasak itself, as the protagonist. I quote the review at length to analyse how it refers back to the world of the novel and highlights the possibilities of transformation offered by the use of space:

> The stage is set as Khasak, with a suggestive sprawling fields on all the three sides, Aliyar's tea shop and Madhavan Nair's stitching centre on each side, Ravi's single-teacher school on the dais, Mollakka and Mai-muna's house in the box-like centre stage and so on. The open space in the middle transforms itself into many in the process of unfolding drama. With a few strokes, Alla Picha Mollakka makes it his madrassa. In the next scene, the minaret is erased by an angry Sivaraman Nair . . . with his feet. It is only one example of the many occasions of natural transformation of settings in the play . . . Nizam Ali makes love with Maimuna and fights with Ravi in the wet soil. Mungamkozhi digs a well in the centre stage and later, gets buried in it. On several occasions, Nizam Ali, Ravi and Maimuna enter in neat white clothes and leave the stage clad in mud . . . The odours of perfume, talcum powder and incense sticks and the reek of gun powder and kerosene fill the stage throughout the narrative.
>
> (Ragesh)

Whilst the use of the space is celebrated for its unique impact at the level of the senses, what is also striking is the stress on the characters as the performance develops more or less all the prominent characters from the novel with each having at least one moment of intensity. This aesthetic, closer to postdramatic, does not erase the original text. Lavender argues that even as some contemporary performances foreground "event-ness," they could "equally entail heightened experiences of dramatic mediation" (87). For Lavender, the shift towards "event-ness and a simultaneous swing away from mimesis, narration and representation" that Lehmann imagined might not have been the necessary direction that contemporary performance practices took, as he highlights how certain performances "depend, structurally, on the coherence provided by texts and intertexts in presenting their own no less cogent worlds" (87). Lavender further argues that "they stage scenes of mimetic representation, albeit framed overtly within eventual production. Whilst there is an emphasis on the *process* of viewing and an *openness* by way of their multi-perspectival mode, there is also a drive to closure and conclusion. In these instances, the production is rendered as a complete entity, a 'finished result'. If these works are postdramatic, they are so in a way that recuperates the dramatic" (87). Let me analyse the specificity of dramatic mediation in *Ithihasam*, which transforms the modernist text to one placed within the contemporary globalisation.

Heteroglossia and contemporary migration

One of the striking aspects of the novel is its use of language, particularly the way in which a single language is inflected with the power and location of the speakers. Whilst Ravi and the upper-caste Madhavan Nair speak in formal Sankritised Malayalam, all other characters in the novel speak in a mixture of Malayalam and Tamil, indicating the localised community status of its speakers. The performance carries forward this perspective. It employs the characters' words from the novel as well as an extra-diegetic narratorial voice that arises in different sequences. The narratorial voice taken from the novel itself uses the formalised Malayalam language. The use of varied Malayalam itself raises the question of polyphony. But the polyphony is not limited to the varied dialects. Instead, as Marvin Carlson argues about stage language and heteroglossia, it needs to be seen as a broader category involving cultures and subcultures (5). Further, the varied cultures and sub-cultures cannot simply be isolated and compartmentalised into distinct categories as they come to the forefront to produce heteroglossia precisely in their intersection. The multiple cultures that one sees in *Ithihasam* include the mainstream ritual practices of Rowthers and Ezhavas, the black magic, and the marginal, localised rituals and beliefs. In the performance, their intensity gets amplified as the varied rituals and practices are staged sometimes one after another in immediate succession. For instance, after seeing a sequence of Naijamali performing black magic rituals to drive away the djinns, the next sequence is a full restaging of the popular Hindu ritual involving the shaman (*velichappadu*) and body suspension, in which one is suspended on hooks piercing one's skin. Yet towards the end of the ritual, the performance swiftly moves to a video projection of an abstract image. What is the intersection of diverging religious practices and their virtual worlds?

The adaptation of the world of heteroglossia raises complex questions of comprehension. To whom does the world of heteroglossia become accessible? Is it to an audience deemed to be "natives" living under conditions of heteroglossia or is it accessible to an audience outside the cultural contexts? In the case of the novel, Mukundan, in fact, ascribes the failure of the English translation to what can be seen as heteroglossia. He argues that "it is impossible to render it in any other language—its language, imageries and subtleties which are culture-specific are not simply translatable" (87). The virtual world constituted in the performance moves away from the question of whether Khasak is too regional/local to be translated to another cultural audience in order to formulate a radically different experience of the regional/local itself in the contemporary moment of globalisation. The global aesthetic of theatre of engagement plays a crucial part in it. But, importantly, it brings to the forefront a new regional world constituted in migration practices. The region of Kerala itself underwent massive changes, attributable in particular to a "Gulf boom" that generated massive out-migration of lower-class and lower-caste labour from Kerala to the Gulf from the 1970s onwards, converting the region into one primarily dependent on repatriation money and quickly being transformed into a consumer regime. Whilst transnational flows have played significant part in the rise of new cultural forms in the region (Parameswaran 2017), ritual practices also assumes a special status due to migration. Rather than being archaic, the mainstream rituals that one sees in *Ithihasam* are ones that have grown in spectacle allowing a new identity articulation in the context of globalisation. Analysing the phenomenon, Osella et al. point to the relationship between Gulf migration and rituals in the region:

> By donating money to local temples and sponsoring public festivals, Gulf migrants have also been able to take on positions of responsibility in the management committees of mainstream temples, often disrupting existing power structures based either on lineage seniority or customary ritual rights. Public religious activities—especially temple festivals—are therefore often local sites of struggles for precedence, prestige and status through which individual and collective/caste projects of social mobility are articulated and given expression.
>
> (118)

The mainstream rituals that we see in *Ithihasam* are, therefore, new identity articulations. The intersection of the Rowther and Ezhava practices, rather than being an abstract experience of the communities constituted in rituals, posits an affirmation of the multiplicity against the violent homogenising tendency of the current Indian mainstream of erasing and "othering" of non-Hindu religions, especially Islam, from the imagination.[2]

Yet even as it presents a world of multiple cultures, the performance is neither a celebration nor a fetishisation of a world of perfect coexistence of multiplicities. Instead, it demonstrates that the non-mainstream rituals and practices, both of Rowthers and Ezhavas, stand against the drive against the standardisation and "cleansing" of religious practices on moral grounds. It is here that those such as Maimuna, with her open sexuality (in love with Naijamali and continuing to have relationships, even after her marriage), stand outside mainstream morality. Wearing a hijab, sitting alone smoking *beedi* after sex, Maimuna signals powerfully that a world exists outside middle-class and religious fundamentalist frameworks of morality.

Conclusion

The present chapter interrogates the adaptation of an iconic modernist text in the global aesthetic of theatre of engagement and looks at how migration can be seen as playing a critical part in the new aesthetic. Lavender foregrounds that one of the ways in which one can contextualise the politics of theatres of engagement is that

it suggests a set of performances that are turned towards their society, deliberately invested in social process, political perspective, matters of import to gathered groups of people. This is a theatre that is socially committed, not necessarily in order to espouse a particular perspective (although it might), but to perform an age-old function: provide a seeing place (*theatron*) where matters of significance are shared communally, and a gathering ground where events are inhabited in common.

(26)

The chapter explores how staging an iconic modernist text written in the late 1960s is not a nostalgic experience of the past. Instead, the dramaturgical intervention that stages multiple cultures in a condition of heteroglossia, presents a new experience that foregrounds the historical transformation of the region through migration. Whilst technology holds a crucial place indicating a new experience of the contemporary as distinct from the earlier theatre of the roots movement, the "event inhabited in common" in the case of *Ithihasam* moves away from a simplistic perspective of secularisation and homogenisation through globalisation. Instead, in *Ithihasam's* dramaturgical intervention, the ritualistic practices that have become reconceived sites of new identity articulation through the investment of the new class of migrant labour is not isolated from the identification elicited by the rise of new media and technology. Against the discourse of Hindutva, the entangled world of Rowthers and Ezhava offers a contemporary world that does not constitute communities in isolation or construct Islam as the "Other". But as heteroglossia, the stage language also does not simply present an empirical and natural status quo; instead, the engagement is one that demands a reconceptualisation of the present and a dialogue because the multiplicities also conflict in challenging the morality of the mainstream shared across communities in a world of globalisation.

Notes

1   Graduating from the Thrissur School of Drama, the director Deepan Sivaraman pursued his Ph.D. in scenography at the Wimbledon College of Arts and is currently working as Associate Professor in Performance Studies at the School of Culture and Creative Expressions, Ambedkar University, New Delhi. Continuing to work as scenographer for other directors, Sivaraman's own directorial works, meantime, include *Spinal Cord* (2009), *Peer Gynt* (2010), *Ubu Roi* (2012), *Project Nostalgia* (2014), *The Cabinet of Dr. Caligari* (2015). For *Ithihasam*, the dramaturgy and scenography is done by Sivaraman himself, while the music is done Chandran Veyyattummal and the cast include Balamani V. K, Aswathy K., Kumar Pariyacheri, Manoj K. U, C. K. Sunil, Tharima K. L, Rajeevan Vellur, C. K. Sudheer, Rajesh Karyan Kuttan, V.K. Originally produced in Trikkaripur by K. M. K. Smaraka Kalasamithi, so far *Ithihasam* has been performed more than fifty times as independent ticketed shows organized by various associations across towns and city-centres in Kerala and in cities such as Bangalore, Bombay, and Jaipur as well as at theatre festivals. For the purpose of this chapter, the descriptions of the performances are taken from the original production I saw in Trikkarippur and the video documentation of the performance that was done as part of the Theatre Olympics. I have referenced the dialogues of the play based on the latter.
2   There has been a conspicuous effort to define India as fundamentally Hindu under the regime of the Bharatiya Janata Party and the current prime minister, who was at the helm in the state of Gujarat when pogroms against Muslims were undertaken in 2002.

Works cited

Bhabha, Homi K. *The Location of Culture*. Routledge, 1994.
Bharucha, Rustom. "Negotiating the 'River': Intercultural Interactions and Interventions." *TDR (1988–)*, vol. 41, no. 3, 1997, pp. 31–38. *JSTOR*, doi:10.2307/1146607.
Carlson, Marvin. *Speaking in Tongues: Languages at Play in the Theatre*. U of Michigan P, 2006.
Chaudhuri, Una. "Beyond a 'Taxonomic Theater': Interculturalism after Postcolonialism and Globalization." *Theater*, vol. 32, no. 1, Jan. 2002, pp. 33–47.
Cheah, Pheng. "Given Culture: Rethinking Cosmopolitical Freedom in Transnationalism." *Boundary 2*, vol. 24, no. 2, 1997, pp. 157–197. *JSTOR*, doi:10.2307/303767.
Gilbert, Helen, and Jacqueline Lo. *Performance and Cosmopolitics: Cross-cultural Transactions in Australasia*. Springer, 2007.
Jayakumar, K. P. "MarichuPoyavarChoottuKathichuKhasakkilethiyathengene?" *Asianet News*, 30 May 2017, www.asianetnews.com/magazine/kp-jayakumar-column-on-khasakinte-ithihasam-a-play-by-deepan-sivaraman.

Kapur, Geeta. "Globalisation and Culture." *Third Text*, vol. 11, no. 39, 1997, pp. 21–38.

Lavender, Andy. *Performance in the Twenty-First Century: Theatres of Engagement*. Routledge, 2016.

Lehmann, Hans-Thies. *Postdramatic Theatre*. Routledge, 2006.

Mee, Erin B. *Theatre of Roots: Redirecting the Modern Indian Stage*. Seagull Books Pvt Ltd, 2008.

Meerzon, Yana. "The Exilic Teens: On the Intracultural Encounters in Wajdi Mouawad's Theatre." *Theatre Research in Canada/RecherchesThéâtrales au Canada*, vol. 30, no. 1_2, Jan. 2009, *journals.lib.unb.ca*, https://journals.lib.unb.ca/index.php/TRIC/article/view/12457.

Mukundan, M. "O.V. Vijayan: Death and Afterlife of a Writer." *Indian Literature*, vol. 49, no. 2, 2005, pp. 85–89.

Osella, Caroline, and Filippo Osella. "Migration and the Commoditisation of Ritual: Sacrifice, Spectacle and Contestations in Kerala, India." *Modern Asian Studies*, vol. 33, no. 4, 1999, pp. 989–1020.

Parameswaran, Ameet. *Performance and the Political: Power and Pleasure in Contemporary Kerala*. Orient Blackswan, 2017.

Ragesh, G. "Staging Khasak, the protagonist." *Manoramaonline*, 4 Apr. 2016, https://english.manoramaonline.com/entertainment/art-and-culture/khasakinte-ithihasam-play-by-deepan-sivaraman-review.html.

Raveendran, P. P. "Translation and Sensibility: The Khasak Landscape in Malayalam and English." *Indian Literature*, vol. 43, no. 3, 1999, pp. 177–186.

Vijayan, O.V. *Khasakkinte Ithihasam*, Kottayam: DC Books, [1969] 1990.

6 On multiple identities and the glue that holds us together

Margareta Sörenson and Jonas Hassen Khemiri

Jonas Hassen Khemiri is one of the most important writers of his generation in Sweden. When his debut novel, *One Eye Red* (*Ett öga rött*), was published in 2003, Khemiri's eccentric and imaginative prose made an enormous impact, reaching an audience far beyond traditional literary circles. The book sold over 200,000 copies in paperback—the most of any book in Sweden in 2004. Khemiri's second novel, *Montecore: The Silence of the Tiger* (*Montecore—en unik tiger*), was awarded the prestigious P.O. Enquist Literary Prize and the Swedish Radio's Award for Best Novel. *Everything I Don't Remember* (*Allt jag inte minns*) was published in 2015 and won Khemiri the prestigious August Prize for Best Swedish Fiction Book of the Year. His forthcoming novel, *The Father Clause* (*Pappaklausulen*), will be published by FSG (United States) and Harvill Secker (United Kingdom) in the spring of 2020.

Khemiri is also a celebrated playwright whose six plays have been performed by over one hundred international companies on stages from Stockholm to Berlin to New York to London. His plays attack deep prejudices about identity, race, and language. He was awarded an Obie Award for his first play, *Invasion!*, which premiered in New York in 2011. *The Hundred We Are* received the Hedda Award for best play in Norway. Khemiri's most recent play, *≈[Almost Equal To]*, premiered at the Royal Dramatic Theatre in Stockholm in October 2014 and has been performed in Germany, Norway, Iceland, Denmark, and the United States. Khemiri's writing has been translated into over 25 languages. In 2017, he became the first Swedish writer to have a short story published in the *New Yorker*.

Even in his early years, Khemiri was fascinated by language, books, and words. He discovered the theatre later, as a student of literature and economics at university. By chance, he happened to go to a theatre performance and was captivated. Novels remain his foremost platform, but theatre is a space for experimenting with time and timing, characters, and the immediacy of the audience's response.

About discovering theatre

Jonas Hassen Khemiri: Since I was a child, books were my thing. I spent endless hours in the library. I had a younger brother who was interested in acting, and in a family, you often divide the world between you and your siblings. So my brother had theatre, and I had books. It took a long time to discover what a stage could be used for. It wasn't until I was in my 20s that I started going to the theatre. I was a student, and in my school, we were allowed to attend performances of shows that were still in development. I could go for free, which was important, as I was a student and didn't have any money, and we could see rehearsals and run-throughs of plays that were not at all polished. We were always waiting for the director to intervene, to yell "cut!" or "let's do a retake" and then finally understood the power of theatre. That tension added something new that I hadn't seen before. Something was created as I was watching it, and all of a sudden, it was obvious why I was supposed to be in that physical space, taking part in that particular story. I went from feeling like an observer to feeling involved. After that, I went to see everything from Strindberg's *A Dream Play*, elegantly directed by Robert Wilson, to experimental plays in small out of the way theatres. I saw dance and performance too, but in the end, I am a language nerd; words are my life buoy.

About how it all started

I studied both literature and economics, but the dreams of becoming a writer started much earlier, beginning with a fascination for books and the way that they could banish time. Literature had the ability to whisper that the reader was not alone in his or her strange ways or rather that the writer and the reader were strange in the same ways and that there were always other possible worlds, realities beyond a boring everyday life full of "you musts" like studying literature or economics. After graduation, I worked part time in a clothing store, part time as a dishwasher, and devoted all my free time to trying to finish my first novel, grandly titled *The Dilemma of the Pond Guard or Ayatollah Is a Title*. At 18, I was sure this novel would change the future of Swedish literature. Now, at 39, I am thankful it was never published. I worked on it for years, then spent six months moving commas. I was terrified to show my text to anyone else. Finally, I sent it to a publisher. In waiting for the dreaded response letter, my text mutated. Suddenly, I saw the too constructed plot. The heavy-handed symbolism. The self-satisfied metaphors. The exaggerated number of penguins. I realised that this was not me writing. This was me trying desperately to write like my writer idols: Nabokov, Duras, and Nas. So, instead of waiting for a response from the publisher, I started a new project which I tried to write purely for my own enjoyment. That, ultimately, became my debut novel, *Ett Öga Rött* (*One Eye Red*), published in 2003.

Since then, I have written four novels and six plays. In the beginning of my career, I remember being frustrated that the time between completing a project and starting to see its faults was so short. Now I try to see this as a sign that I haven't stagnated. At least not yet.

About the novel and the first play

After *Ett öga rött* was published, I was asked to write a play by Benny Fredriksson, now sadly deceased, who was the head of Stadsteatern, the city theatre in Stockholm. At our first meeting, I had the impression that he wanted a specific story, that there were certain aspects of myself that he wanted me to relate. My first reaction was to turn down the commission because I didn't feel free to write as I wished. But I went away from that meeting and started thinking about a famous but now somewhat forgotten Swedish Romantic playwright and novelist called Carl Jonas Love Almqvist whom I had been reading at the time. I emailed Benny to say that if I were going to write a play it would be about the "1,000 faces of Abulkasem", and that became the basis for my first play, *Invasion!*. The play starts out with a short excerpt from Almqvist's play Senora Luna. Some young people rebel against the historic language, steal the name Abulkasem from Almqvist, and start filling it with their own meaning. Abulkasem becomes a word that can mean anything, a limitless word, signifying a threat to some, and a self-empowerment tool for others. In a way, it's a play about people trying and failing to free themselves from categorisation.

I was very happy to write for the theatre, and it was amazing to see how the play changed when it started attracting a new kind of audience. But I see writing books as my main job. In Swedish, we have a word, *växelbruk* (crop rotation). Every year or two, you change the grains to renew the soil. I think I use theatre to experiment, just as I write short stories or film scripts, but the grain that I need to survive is the novels. I need to have a novel on the go to be happy.

About the latest play

My latest play is called ≈ [*Almost Equal To*]. It premiered at the National Dramatic Theatre and was originally written as part of a project on Mary Shelley. The dramaturg basically asked me to write something about Frankenstein. I went home and started thinking of power, of what happens when we create something and then lose control over it. And so it became a play about contemporary economics instead of monsters. It was great fun to write about capitalism, not only its disadvantages—that would have been too easy—but also the allure of money, the power aspect, and how liberating it can be to get a raise.

The play premiered before the somewhat bourgeois audience of the Royal Dramatic Theatre and their laughter was often very uncomfortable, which I found interesting. The play was extended and started attracting an audience that normally does not go to this theatre, and then the text changed gradually during its run and became better and darker, because the audience were not laughing at the same time. The fiction that was created onstage managed to create some interesting friction in the audience.

About different forms

Everything that I cannot do in the novel that I can do in the play intrigues me. For instance, the ability to control time. It is tricky to do that in a book, but in the theatre, I can have long pauses if I want them, or we can lock the doors to force the audience to stay. The magic of theatre is that you have the physicality, you have the bodies and voices present that you as the audience have to react to—and react to weirdly in some cases—but what I think drove me back to the novel form is that there is a peculiar intimacy when you are forced to create the body in your mind and hear the voice in your own head. The novel *Everything I Don't Remember* found its form after having written a few plays where I was longing for the freedom to force the words to be only words. And the whole novel circles around that. How different might a certain sentence be when the reader has to decide who is saying it? It is not always 100 percent certain who is speaking. When someone says, "I loved him", and it is not obvious who is speaking then the meaning can change dramatically. I think this going back and forth between different modes of expression—the novel and the play—they seep into each other. It is also a way of keeping writing fresh and fascinating.

About the open letter

Margareta Sörenson: In 2013, Khemiri wrote an open letter to Sweden's Minister of Justice at the time, Beatrice Ask, a conservative. The letter noted that Swedish citizens of very different backgrounds are not treated equally due to the fact that some people with power, such as politicians, policemen, or journalists, often see them as Other—part of a different group, referring to them as immigrants, even though they are Swedish.

Jonas Hassen Khemiri: The play, *I Call My Brothers*, and the letter share some themes, mainly because I have always been interested in how groups are being created, with the political use of the idea of an outsider, someone who is not part of this group. I think the letter was so widely admired in Sweden because a lot of people—no matter their background—could relate to the feeling of not being seen as "real" citizens.

More about the letter

Margareta Sörenson: The letter was also shared, translated, and published internationally, as in the *New York Times*. In a personal tone, the writer discussed critically a new instruction for policemen to find undocumented persons. Anyone looking "foreign" could be asked for identification without any suspicion or other cause. Khemiri was not the only one to protest, but his open letter took a giant step in provoking a public debate about the issue; the guidelines for policemen were stopped a short time later.

Jonas Hassen Khemiri: I wrote it in response to a radio interview made by the minister of justice. When Swedish citizens complained about being racially profiled, our minister answered by comparing these worried citizens with paranoid ex-cons. In the letter, I ask Beatrice Ask to switch bodies and memories with me. If I entered her body, I would understand male privilege, and if she entered my body, she would remember being followed in stores by security guards, being stopped in customs at airports, being stopped and put in the back seat of police cars, for no reason whatsoever. These things happened to me when I was growing up. For a long time, I stopped myself from writing about these events because I had friends from poorer backgrounds who had much worse experiences with the police. But, finally, I realised that it's a very efficient strategy for people in power to silence any demands for justice and equality by pointing to someone who has it "worse". So I wrote the text, and it went viral. A lot of people could relate to the feeling of not being seen as part of the official myth of their respective country, no matter their ethnic background or sexual orientation. And maybe it also spread because so many countries are in this position of not knowing who they are. What is the glue that holds us together?

About being called "immigrant"

I don't write about immigrants. I write about contemporary Sweden. My novels are filled with different people of different ages and different backgrounds. There are many different ways to describe them: they search for everlasting love; they meet and fall in love; they are betrayed. And, yes, they also have a father. And a mother. And they are from different countries. It is up to the reader to decide which of these attributes offers the most insights into someone's personality.

About the practical side of theatrical work

When I write a play, I normally attend one rehearsal and the opening. No more. I am not involved in casting. My primary goal is to write interesting stories. In order to write well, I have to be honest and specific, and it would feel bizarre and fake to write about contemporary Sweden in the old "blue-eyed" way and not to include people from different backgrounds. To me, it's just a natural consequence of trying to tell stories that matter. Then, in order to cast the plays, the directors have to find the best possible actors, and naturally, they look for people whose thoughts and experiences relate to the script. I'm proud that many of the actors who started out in my plays are now performing roles that are not linked in any way to a specific political movement.

I have great faith in my hearing, a strong sense for the sound of the characters' voices, but I rarely imagine what the plays will look like. One of the best productions of my first play *Invasion!* turned out to be in Hamburg at the Thalia Theatre using a minimalistic set. The scenography could not have cost more than two euros. It was fantastic. The lack of props forced the actors to focus on the words, and they really made the text sing.

My general feeling is that something good happens when a text is "kidnapped" by a director and collides with his or her vision. If the play works, it can withstand the changes. I never comment on the aesthetics. The only comments I make are about sound. "I think she should be sadder when she says that", for example; or "that should be lighter"; or "that should be darker". This is because my creative process is all about listening to voices. Reading Anna Karenina, I cannot fully understand why Anna is sad about not dancing the last mazurka of the evening. But a good text makes references come alive. I don't need to know anything about mazurkas to understand Anna's sadness at having been stood up. The same goes for theatre.

I never think of future translations or performances in other countries when I write. If I did, I would be haunted by someone else gazing at me.

Books let you decide everything as a reader, which is wonderful. A play already presents images and actors. To me, it is important that a production onstage invites the audience to be a co-creator. If not, I feel like falling asleep. When theatre is at its best, it lets you feel a bit like the reader of a book. It transforms you into an active participant.

About writing multiple identities

I have never really understood the idea of a "true" self. One identity that is more real than the other ones. Maybe that's why I keep coming back to the theme of identity in my writing. I find it rather fascinating that we have so many potential identities within us at the same time and that we are able to switch amongst them with lightning speed when asked (or forced) by the outside world. Here are some of the identities that I have tried on today: father, boyfriend, Stockholmer, man, car-owner, coffee-drinker, subway-traveller, eldest brother, book reader, Kendrick Lamar-listener, and, now, sitting in a library answering these questions—writer. If I had to choose one of these identities, I guess it would be writer, simply since that is what I spend most time doing (or worrying about not doing).

About the writing process and reviews

I find myself writing best when I lead a maximally boring life. Meaning: leaving my kids at day care and then isolating myself in my writing studio south of Stockholm. Paradoxically, I need those hours of complete isolation and focus on writing to feel somewhat connected to the outside world.

I have always seen the positive reactions to my writing as an encouragement to fail better and, I hope, be more courageous in the next project.

Part II

On inter- and intra-
multilingualism of migration

7 On multilinguality, decolonisation and postmigrant theatre

A conversation between Azadeh Sharifi and Laura Paetau

In our ongoing personal and theoretical conversation, we—a theatre scholar (Azadeh Sharifi) and a sociologist and dramaturg (Laura Paetau)—discuss art, academia, activism, and everyday life. We are particularly interested in intersectional feminism and postmigrant theatre. For this contribution, we are focusing on the queer performance group Frutas from Berlin. The group consists of the performers Jair Luna, Simon(e) Paetau and Iury Trojaborg, the dramaturg Laura Paetau, and the set and stage designer Michaela Muchina. In their performance *Frutas Afrodisíacas*,[1] which premiered in June 2016, Jair, Simon(e), and Iury perform the characters Jaira del Caribe, Simoneta mal Pagada, and Lubrica de la Pasión.[2]

In our conversation on *Frutas Afrodisíacas*, we look into the strategies of resistance and empowerment which are implemented through deconstructing stereotypes projected on the Latinx body, performative decolonisation (or as it is called in the performance, "*Reculonisación*") and multilinguality against an imposed German monolingualism.

Laura

Have you ever danced in the tropics?
With that hazy lazy
Like, kind of crazy
Like South American Way
Ai, ai, ai, ai
Have you ever kissed in the moonlight
In the grand and glorious
Gay notorious
South American Way?

(Frutas 2016)

The opening sequence invites the audience to a theatre bar that resembles Café Anal, the famous queer bar in West Berlin in the 1980s. It is also an imagined South American space with a video projected in loop on several screens. These show white sand beaches in the Caribbean, mountains, rivers, and the green Amazon forest. We see parrots, fruits, women dancing, and hear a deep voice announcing: "Colombia. The only risk is wanting to stay" (Colombiatravel 2012).

The three performers run around, cleaning and getting dressed. Suddenly, music begins to play, and the three line up and start to dance. They smile, sing, and share plastic fruits. From there, *Frutas* takes the audience on a journey through autobiographical and fictionalised stories of the performers.

Azadeh: The performance is rich with layers and complex intertextual references that unravel onstage—and in the imagination of the audience. One of the more prominent aspects, at least for me as a theatre scholar, is the way that othering and stereotypisation are dealt with in the performance through different dramaturgical formats. One of these formats is the use of ongoing images of the Latinx within Western media, which contain an exoticised, sexualised, and colonised representation. I was wondering how you dealt on a dramaturgical and performative level with these stereotypes and how you transformed them into theatrical moments of resistance and empowerment.

Laura: In the rehearsals, we discussed what kind of stereotypes of Latinas exist and how to translate and dissect them in the performance. Iury Trojaborg introduced Carmen Miranda and the song "The South American Way", sung by Marisa Monte in Portuguese and English. I quoted it earlier in the text. Carmen Miranda was a Portuguese-born Brazilian samba singer and dancer who became the first famous Latin American in the United States to perform the Latina stereotype. She wore fruits on her hat. She was once the highest paid woman in Hollywood but could never escape the image of a constantly smiling, flamboyant singer known as the Brazilian bombshell. During the rehearsals, Iury worked on a reinterpretation of Miranda's body language and movements, referring to her both in admiration and as a tragic figure. The other two performers, who got to know Carmen Miranda through the rehearsal process, chose different paths to relate to her. Simon(e) Paetau searched for modern versions of the stereotype he could relate to. He created his personal version of Sofia Vergara. In my reading, Sofia Vergara is a contemporary take on the Latina stereotypes in U.S. show business that Carmen Miranda introduced. Jair Luna, on the other hand, refused to engage with it completely; he did not even want to re-enact Carmen Miranda with a critical distance and went in the opposite direction. He chose to embody a German tourist, passionately lip-syncing Carmen Miranda's song and expressing his *discovery* of the Latin American way of life. I understand his approach as a strategy of refusal. Their individual interpretation of the Latina stereotype was presented to the audience in this first scene. By using symbolic parts of their costumes—the long hair and the hat with fruits as well as the blond wig as counterpart (Figure 7.1)—the performers remind us of this stereotypical image at the beginning of the performance or refuse to represent them.

Another important take on the reflection of othering and categorisation involves the internalised colonial gaze made visible through a TV show. Here the self-perception which is set by the internalised colonial system is made visible through the split into two figures: Jair Luna as TV presenter and Simon(e) Paetau as Jaira del Caribe. The TV reporter asks Jaira del Caribe very personal questions but is actually more concerned with her looks, her hair, and her shoes. She is indifferent to Jaira's responses and suddenly stops the interview without giving Jaira del Caribe a proper opportunity to present herself.

In my view, this scene shows the different levels of psychological and epistemic violence we carry inside that make us feel less worthy and relevant. The internalised colonial order is visualised through the power struggle between the TV reporter and Jaira del Caribe.

Azadeh: I also recognise this scene as crucial to dismantle the power of the colonial gaze. And I think that W.E.B. Du Bois's notion of double-consciousness,

Figure 7.1 Simon(e) Paetau as Simoneta Malpagada, Iury Trojaborg as Lubrica de la Pasión, Jair Luna as Jaira del Caribe. *Frutas Afrodisíacas* directed by Jair Luna, Simon(e) Paetau, Iury Trojaborg. Studio Я, Maxim Gorki Theater and Ballhaus Naunynstrasse. July 2016

Photo Credit: Ospina 2016

"this sense of always looking at one's self through the eyes of others" (Du Bois 1989: 5), is rendered into the performance. In the scene, double-consciousness is perceptible through the split of the characters but also through the hierarchy of what is important and what is not. The notion of Spivak's *epistemic violence* (Spivak 1988) is translated into who may speak – namely, the TV presenter and her dismissive behaviour towards Jaira del Caribe and the impossibility of self-representation of the colonised subject. But by doing so, the performance creates an actual space of decolonisation, extracting the internalised gaze of the coloniser and putting it literally outside of the subject's body. There is another crucial scene where the colonial order that is put on colonised bodies is made apparent through a ritual of cleaning—or, as you call it, *Reculonización*.

Laura: In the scene *Reculonización*, Jaira del Caribe reenacts a commercial show for housewives. Jaira uses a long brush as a cleaning object and an antique gramophone as the object which needs to be cleaned. She explains, "Like Critóbal Colón we drive along the coast, cleaning it from all the bad, dirt and black" (Frutas 2016). In performance, this scene was spoken in Spanish. She cleans the gramophone from the outside in and points right to the centre of it.

> When we come to the center, we push and push and clean again— *out with the dirt!* We want to have it clean and white—like our anus. Like our history, our anus is facing backwards. But we have to turn it around. Face it and show it to the world.
>
> (Frutas 2016)

This scene can be read as a de-colonising performative moment in which the cleaning of the anus is a metaphor for the ongoing process of colonisation in the postcolonial present. The word Re-*culo*-nización that Jaira del Caribe constantly uses has its roots in the Spanish word *culo*, meaning anus, and through the performative act, a queering takes place.

Azadeh: The queer reading enables us, the audience, to reflect on how heteronormativity and the colonial order is imposed as a fixed frame. This particular scene visualises a shift in the story, challenging the power dynamics of the colonial structure. More than that, it creates a new perspective from which we can re-read history, which I feel is essential for the process of decolonisation. There is another essential layer, the linguistic level, at which the process of decolonisation is woven into the performance. I find it fascinating how multilingualism is established onstage. All languages are considered equal and the colonial hierarchy is opposed.

For me, multilinguality is a prominent dramaturgical strategy in the performance. I would identify three categories of how multilinguality is inserted in the performance: first, as a tool of articulation and communication (logos) that generates different forms of inclusion and exclusion; second, as a counter-strategy against the colonial order, challenging the colonial hierarchy that is imposed on non-European languages; and, finally, as a device of appropriation of space, time, and historical and current events.

Laura: We used four languages in the performance: Spanish is the first and second language of three of the artists and the common language of the group. German is the language of migration, with the local reference to Berlin. Portuguese is another native language of one of the performers, and English is the common language used by the international production team. During the creative process, we focused on how to use these four languages. I discussed this issue intensely during the weekly dramaturgy meetings at the Ballhaus Naunynstrasse theatre. I asked, How do we create a performance with four languages and translate amongst them? Should we use surtitles or leaflets? We decided against these options and solved the problem at the level of the performance itself. The moment of translation turned from a simple technical issue into a significant dramaturgical decision: the choice of language to be placed in the centre of each action or scene was the result of dramaturgical negotiation and was presented onstage through performative means.

We also worked with the hierarchy of accents within a language, like in the scene with the TV reporter, when Jaira del Caribe speaks with a Spanish rather than a Colombian accent, because within the colonial order, a supposed Spanish heritage is considered of higher value and class privilege.

In the scene *Reculonización*, there is a crucial moment regarding linguistic translation. Simoneta mal Pagada translates the text of Jaira del Caribe from Spanish into German. The flowery language Jaira uses becomes bureaucratic, static, and stiff. Simoneta's German sounds emotionless, a comment on the difference between Spanish and German that does not allow the same play with words. This came up in the rehearsal when we were trying out different ways of translating but couldn't find a way to express the word "anus" within "Re-*culo*-nisation" in German. So we moved the translation to a different dramaturgical and symbolic level. As Jaira del Caribe explains the process of re-*culo*-nisation, Simoneta mal Pagada's version includes different references, like Bernhard von Bülow's 1897 statement, "We secure our place in the sun" (*Platz an der Sonne*), a euphemistic phrase about imperialism and colonial expansion for the German nation. In this particular scene, we underline the different positionalities that a white and a brown performer bring to the stage, and we used three layers of translation: the linguistic, the cultural context, and the positionalities they represent.

Azadeh: The way you and the performers deal with translation, I am reminded of Walter Benjamin's "The Task of the Translator", where he describes translation as a form and discusses the issues of translatability

(Benjamin 2002: 254). On a very different level, there is a correlation between the imagined reality of the performance and the reality of the audiences. Multilinguality is not only part of the everyday life of migrants and their children, and therefore is Germany's present, but in fact is also part of Germany's past. There are at least four officially recognised minorities in Germany with their own languages and cultures. But within the hegemonic narrative of Germanness,[3] there is the proposition of monolingualism where German is constituted the only language. So when within the performance a space of continuous multilinguality is created through a simultaneity and equivalence of four languages, it resonates—and here I refer to Naika Foroutan (2014) and Erol Yildiz (2014)—with the current postmigrant German society. If we want to challenge the narrative of Germanness—one language, one narrative, and one heritage—we should do it by claiming the space through multilinguality and multiperspectivity.

Laura: Our performance is certainly not made for one audience. Performances probably never are, but especially not in our case. Multiplicity takes place on different levels, and language is one of them. Differences are negotiated within the performance and also between the performers and the audience. And we kept the *différance* of the languages, with all the cultural references and performative aspects they carry. We created moments of visibility for each of them. The performance doesn't give preference to any one understanding and no language is subordinated to another, offering a one-dimensional translation. Through its multilinguality comes a shift of language and, therefore, meaning. This is what I understand to be the dramaturgy of migration.

Azadeh: Here I agree with you on your understanding of the dramaturgy of migration. And that is why in my opinion the performance is extraordinary, an approach I rarely see within the German theatre. For me, it is necessary in order to formulate a postmigrant and postcolonial critique on German theatre and the German society. I want to end our conversation with an optimistic view of the possible futures that we scholars and artists of colour are initiating. As Simoneta mal Pagada says at the end of the performance, "Let's keep on kicking up the dust from the ground. /And here we are but in heels!" (Frutas 2016).

Notes

1 The premiere of *Frutas Afrodisiacas* was in June 2016 at Studio Я, Maxim Gorki Theatre.
2 The characters are performed in drag and therefore we use the pronoun *she*.
3 Following the definition of Alberto Alesina and Bryony Reich on "nation-building" (Alesina and Reich 2015), I understand Germanness as an essential part of the German nation building project. After World War II, there have been

attempts to dis-identify from the German history of racism, antisemitism, and white supremacy, but essentially the core of Germany's national identity is still tied to the ethno-nationalistic construction that began in the eighteenth century and is tightly connected to the place of the state and the city theatres in it (Sosulski 2016).

Works cited

Ahmed, Sara. *Living a Feminist Life*. Duke UP, 2017.

Alesina, Alberto, and Bryony Reich. "Nation-Building." *Scholars at Harvard*, Feb. 2015, scholar.harvard.edu/files/alesina/files/nation_building_feb_2015_0.pdf.

Benjamin, Walter. "The Task of the Translator." *Walter Benjamin: Selected Writings, 1: 1913–1926*, edited by Marcus Bullock and Michael W. Jennings, 5th ed., Harvard University Press, 2004, pp. 253–263.

Colombiatravel. "Colombia, the Only Risk Is Wanting to Stay. Video Country." *YouTube*, 9 Aug. 2012, www.youtube.com/watch?v=F8y4gBz4bR0.

Du Bois, W.E.B. *The Souls of Black Folk*. Penguin, 1989.

Foroutan, Naika et al., eds., *Deutschland postmigrantisch I. Gesellschaft, Religion, Identität. Erste Ergebnisse*. Humboldt-Universität zu Berlin, 2014.

"Frutas Afrodisiacas." Performance premiere by Jair Luna, Simon(e) Paetau, and Iury Trojaborg, Frutas, 23 June 2016, Ballhaus Naunynstrasse, Berlin.

Sosulski, Michael J. *Theatre and Nation in Eighteenth-Century in Germany*. Routledge, 2016.

Spivak, Gayatri Chakravorty. "Can the subaltern speak?" *Marxism and the Interpretation of Culture*, edited by Cary Nelson and Lawrence Grossberg, Macmillan, 1988.

Yildiz, Erol, and Marc Hill, eds. *Nach der Migration. Postmigrantische Perspektiven jenseits der Parallelgesellschaft*. Transcript, 2014.

8 Representing the migrant body and performing displacement

Contemporary Indian feminist interventionist ecology

Indu Jain

The post-independence theatre milieu in India, especially in the capital city of Delhi, was concerned with constructing a national theatre that would be representative of a national community (Jain 2017). What this theatre tried to do was produce ideal citizen-actor-artists exhibiting the vision of the benevolent state. In his book *Speaking in Tongues: Languages at Play in the Theatre* that expounds on heteroglossic experimentation in theatre, Marvin Carlson points out that this possibility was due to "the decline of both the nationalist and the colonialist projects in their attempt to delegitimize and silence minority voices that challenged and potentially subverted their hegemony" (17). In the Indian theatrical context, this challenge to the patriarchal, hegemonic, and post-independence national canon came from women directors who emerged in the capital in the 1980s. Amongst the most avant-garde voices to emerge, it was Anamika Haksar who through her gendered sensibility and her training in socialist dramaturgy from the Soviet Institute of Theatre Arts in Moscow (1982–1988) not only moved beyond essentially monoglossic productions but also shone the spotlight on minority voices like those of displaced tribal communities and silenced Dalit identities. Migrant tribal communities in India are forced to lead a nomadic existence on the fringes of society due to economic deprivation, social-legal ostracisation, and coercive displacement. These marginalised groups have remained primarily outside mainstream modes of politics of representation, particularly a theatre that has come to be associated with a middle-class urban cultural practice.

In this chapter, I propose that feminist directors like Haksar deliberately seek to present subject matter that does not conform to conventional patriarchal discourse, thus opening up a space for resistance by depicting these subaltern identities. The chapter will explore how her accentuation of sensorial things and soundscapes of area and fluid imagery provoke her actors to focus on their own particular regional identities to bring forward a worldview of multiple perspectives through the language of their bodies in performance. It will specifically focus on Haksar's landmark production *Ucchaka* (2008)[1] and her recent improvisational theatre and installation work, *Composition on Water* (2016).[2] *Ucchaka* is based on Laxman Gaikwad's autobiographical novel, *Uchalaya/The Branded* (1987), which brings to light the trials and tribulations of the *Uchalaya*, a wandering tribe for whom stealing was a primary vocation. Individuals from this tribe do not have a sense of belonging; they are always in a state of being refugees who are made invisible by the very society they inhabit. By virtue of their caste, class and a regressive history of being seen as fringe inhabitants, criminals, hostile, and a threat to the mainstream, they are seen as strangers. Through the depiction of the migrant figure's fears, anxieties, habitat, survival, and livelihood through the abject body, Haksar propels these narratives into the space of middle-class civil society, thereby giving visibility to the concept of "stranger-danger" (Ahmed 2000: 19).

A peregrination from personal to political

Haksar's political inclination and personal life trajectory have contributed to and have had a deep influence on her engagement with the subject matter of her productions. She belongs to the community of Kashmiri Pandits, who are a politically targeted and vulnerable minority in the Indian population. They are a non-Muslim minority group with a history of undergoing forced conversions and migration. In the recent past, they have been forced to flee the Kashmir valley by the terror campaigns seeking to establish an Islamic State.[3] Haksar did not experience the struggles that this community faced directly but as an artist is an embodied signifier of the ethnic cleansing in the country and one who often sees herself engaged with the figure of the *Other*. There is a fair amount of information as well as literature in explosive language available on the Dalit life and on those who migrate due to a number of factors. This information is also perceived by urban theatregoers in India through government discourse and tends to reach them by percolating through a biased media. However, in terms of representation and concretising that reality onstage, there is a big gap. Following Emma Cox's suggestion that we need to pay attention to the politics of emotion in order to perceive the category of the subaltern/noncitizenship as affectively constituted (8), Haksar presents a human story, not just a compendium of statistics and sound bites in her work. The kind of emotions that her work generates, especially through the dexterous use of the performing body onstage, leads to a different kind of audience immersion and association than that produced by official narratives.

Staging the embodied nature of subjectivity: the play of language and movement

Both performances under discussion are adaptations from works written in an Indian regional language, Marathi. However, the primary language for the main action of the plays is Hindi. What is important to me is that Haksar is not adhering to any homogeneous language code between the actors and the intended audience. The performers often break into Marathi in *Uchhaka* and into English along with Hindi in *Composition on Water*, elucidating a powerful theatrical heteroglossia. In both performances, the actors are from different cultural and linguistic backgrounds. I propose that an intercultural experimentation of this kind was possible for Haksar because of her years of engagement with the multilingual, multiregional, and disparate caste student constituency at the National School of Drama and the feminist interventions she undertook through her pedagogical strategies.

In *Uchhaka*, the female actor playing Laxman in one scene is seen squatting under a big dinner table where those from the privileged classes of society are enjoying a sumptuous meal. The dissimilitude becomes even more poignant when the "monologistic semiotic model" (Carlson 20) is severed as she narrates her agony in Marathi. Similarly, in the midst of a monologue that another actor is delivering in English in *Composition on Water*, a man cursing the moneyed and upper-caste oppressors starts using invectives in the vernacular.

These deviations from the primary mode of enunciation are also a conscious tool used by Haksar to delineate the divided self of the migrant figure. However, her real contribution to this representation is done through the stylised movements of the performing bodies. It is not done in a simple analogous binary, but by presenting what I would describe as the polyphony of body languages. As an alternate to varying dialects, speech forms, and tone inflections, I propose that for Haksar heterogeneity in the medium of communication is more in the performing body onstage. The realignment of body and word onstage, that is the text, is (re) authored by the specifics of the body onstage. "My work in theatre is mostly based on movements, poetry, and visual imagery within the text" Haksar explains. "It has redefined, for me, realism from the very stereotypical perspective. I am completely mesmerised by the coordination of body, movement and text. For me, it is a holistic form of theatre" (Haksar, personal interview).

Haksar displaces and breaks from the traditional representations of the body onstage. Her male predecessors, such as Ebrahim Alkazi,[4] made use of the actor's immersion in character, a technique that generated respective sympathy amongst the audience, to merge the language of the body and the spoken language of the character to create an illusion of coherence. Haksar, on the other hand, creates a constructive disengagement of the speaking body and its signifiers. Her *Composition on Water* is an apt example that can best be elaborated upon with the Brechtian theory of Gestus. It is an adaptation of the poetry of Namdeo Dhasal, who was a Marathi writer and a Dalit activist from Maharashtra.[5] In his writings, he drew attention to the circumstances which those deprived of their rights from birth have to endure and about the contradictory reality of the everyday and the "abject" world that the downtrodden inhabit.[6] Haksar brings the pain, anger, and ancestral and present humiliation faced by the figure of the *Other* to the fore through her actor's body in *Composition on Water*. Here, she moves from the proscenium stage to a more intimate space of connection with the audience. It is like a promenade performance where the audience members are free to move and even pass by whilst the actors perform. Her focus here is much more on the affective engaging experience facilitated for the viewers. In elaborating upon the efficacy of affect in theatre, Andy Lavender states,

> It is by way of being sensation-oriented that the work moves from concept into consumption and thereby (for the spectator) into conception. Every artwork proposes a felt response. A form of communicability is the key, something passing from one to the other. This something can be specified only as sensation. It is a zone of indetermination, of indiscernibility . . . this is what is called an *affect*.
>
> (162)

By making use of the psychophysical theatrical trope where the inner and outer worlds come together onstage, Haksar enables a translation of the embodied performative vocabulary into the potential agency of the affective theatrical gestures. The powerless in Haksar's play are confined within a boundary marked by a dirty water drain onstage overflowing with sludge and poverty. They are reduced to an extreme bare life with minimalist means for survival. In *Composition for Water*, they are denied clean drinking water, which is a universal desideratum, and are shown dying of thirst. The performance features two water sources, a fresh cascading wall of water and a rusted drain pipe spewing dirty water, serving to structure water as a metaphor for class, hygiene, and purity. Bodies cringing with thirst, wretched with years of subjugation, frantically digging mud in search of a drop of water, all present a strong visual image to the audience. In order to bring this out from her actors, she made them take a drop of water in a bottle cap and release it into their dry parched throats. The experience of thirst, of stepping into that embodied consciousness, was facilitated through this and several other somatic exercises.

To show her non-unified subjects, Haksar breaks the "rules" of what happens to the speaking body onstage. She employs the use of audience-addressed monologues to downplay any linear narrative form. Patrice Pavis's comments are apropos to a greater understanding of this monologic speech, as he describes Gestus as the radical splitting of the two elements:

> Instead of fusing logos and gestuality in an illusion of reality, the gestus radically cleaves the performance into two blocks: the shown (the said) and the showing (the saying). Discourse no longer has the form of a homogeneous block; it threatens at any moment to break away from its enunciator.
>
> (Pavis 95)

In the performance, the characters reflect their brokenness, their thirst, their angst, and their misery, which is inevitable in their repressive social environment in the gestic self-narrated discourse of Brechtianism. An angry spirit of their ancestors suddenly rises from the mud structure to display its exasperation and struggle of thought through a gestic monologue. There is a halt in the continuity of action and the voice, both bodied and textual, that is appropriate for the enactment of multiple subject positions. Here the language "originates from" the body of the speaking subject (Cixous 253). The actors dressed in the same basic pastel coloured clothes move in a lyrical rhythm interspersed by sudden bursts of narrative speech in more than one language.

The communication through the performing bodies onstage is extended to the imagery used as part of Haksar's scenographic innovation. She uses the image of Buddha to bring forth an opportune amalgamation of tradition and contemporary thought. However, an overturning and deconstructing of the popular visual of the image reinvents tradition here. Buddha, the "enlightened one" in most forms of representations, is presented as a calm meditative vision who has attained *nirvana*. Haksar shows three forms of the Buddha image. We see an emaciated Buddha, in front of whom a thirst-ridden body of an actor sits with anger, making contortions with his body. Buddha here is suffering along with people. Then we see a dying Buddha made out of mud, *Ananthasayanam*. All that he sees as he travels is the death of this land, the underprivileged distressed and racked with pain. And, finally, an inflated balloon Buddha in the meditative posture is placed in front of the fresh water wall at the back. This unstable and air-filled installation deflates slowly into the performance in coordination with the actors' bodies and begins to shrink as their thirst escalates.

The image of an emaciated Buddha also appears in *Ucchaka*, serving a similar purpose. By reinventing the scenography, Haksar's performances present not a functional stage setting but a space that is productive of the change being effected. The investigated living spaces are shaped by people and are ever shifting in *Ucchaka*. As a pedagogue, Haksar emphasises the importance of "knowing yourself". Whilst rehearsing *Uchhaka*, Haksar and her actors met actual pickpockets from the *Uchalaya* tribe. She made her actors do various exercises to learn the art of pickpocketing, to focus on their eyes, stealth movements, etc., so as to devise a new language for the stage to depict the experiences and lives of this nomadic community. Her actors too were a group of people with multilingual and multicultural back-grounds. She worked extensively on the concept of space with her students. How are spaces inhabited and tabooed to these tribes? For example, she made a Brahmin student enact the role of the Dalit body, ridden with infe-riority, and asked, How does it feel to be disempowered? Her focus was on breath awareness and how the body can shrink under the menacing gaze of the observer. To work on these experiences, the actors were asked to run on the edges of the stage, climbing and jumping to immerse themselves physi-cally into the state of living on the margins.

With an eye for minutiae, Haksar gives a powerful rendition to the every-day lives of these tribal migrants. Their manner of eating, the orchestration of thefts, their exclusion from the performativity of religious rituals, and dream sequences of their deaths all constitute the perceptions of identity. The mouth of a big circular drain pipe (see Figure 8.1), half immersed in dirt and mud,

Figure 8.1 Vipin as actor 1, Joy as actor 2. Ucchaka. Directed by Anamika Haksar. 2008. Abhimanch, National School of Drama, Delhi

Credit: Photo by Anamika Haksar

occupies the predominant space of the performance arena, serving as the intimate domestic space that the innocent subjects inhabit.

The performance arena/space becomes a central point where the tortured, violated, and broken bodies represent their intensified emotional state. Throughout the play, performing and moving bodies enter and exit through the arena's entrance. They struggle and their contorted bodies depict the desire to break through the interstices of the unbreachable caste-class divide and hegemonic power structures. The legal machinery of the state treats them as noncitizens. I use the term noncitizens to point towards the deprivation and violation of basic civil rights faced at the hands of the police on an everyday basis. The play shows their unrealised yearnings through a montage of moving bodies choreographed to the beats of drums: there is a woman being held by her *saree* and beaten up and a man with his back bandaged and his wound being ripped open by another who brutally rips off the tape leaving him exposed. There are also other men who strip to their underwear and are beaten by the police.

In order to survive the "normative" violence of their environment, the pickpockets in *Ucchaka* take recourse to self-injury and pain endurance strategies. As the play begins, we see a group of actors moving in circles around a big blade positioned centre stage, worshipping and venerating it. For them, it is the blade that will get food on their plates. As these pickpockets hide these blades deep within their mouth, they often end up lacerating the inside of their mouths. The complex dynamics of (re)presenting the bodies in pain and of watching them represented onstage is where the performing space becomes a generative site of encountering and reanimating that which is rendered invisible by the inflexible supremacist sovereignty, caste, and economic hierarchy. Haksar's satire becomes much more scathing when Laxman's father asks him to recite what he learned in school and he starts to sing the national anthem. She also punctures the inflated idea of the democratic nation-state in a later scene in which video projections of various news channels are shown juxtaposed to the tired bodies onstage. This image further humiliates the tribal migrant communities of India by portraying them as a nuisance and a peril to the common man. Haksar shows bodies working in the factory with vacuous faces staring glassy-eyed at the audience. Their bodies give up under the brutal working conditions, and their consciousness is shredded by the lack of any sense of belonging. A white shiny object, cylindrical in shape, descends upon the stage like a hanging spectre above the actors' bodies (see Figure 8.2).

It is constantly rotating, making a whirring sound, whilst the mill labourers imitate the rotating movement in a freestyle dance. The monotony, the never-ending drudgery, the feeling of alienation finds its visual equivalence in it. Thereafter, when Laxman manages somehow to get an education and comes back to his hometown, he now appears dressed in a shirt and

Figure 8.2 Third year NSD students as mill workers. Ucchaka. Directed by Anamika
Haksar. 2008. Abhimanch, National School of Drama, Delhi

Credit: Photo by Anamika Haksar

full pants, his condition of in-betweenness underlined by this contrasting
change in his clothes.

Sara Ahmed talks about how the cultural politics of emotions creates *Others* by aligning some bodies within a community and marginalising other
bodies. In her chapter on the performativity of disgust, she asks,

> What does it mean to feel "utter disgust"? Why do some things seem
> more disgusting than others? Are we necessarily disgusted by the same
> things and can we recognise when another is "plainly disgusted" by
> what they do with their bodies?
>
> (Ahmed 2014: 82)

Throughout the performance, we hear pejorative tags like *bhangi, chuda*,
and *suar khane wala* used to address the *Uchalaya* people with an emotion
of utter disgust. The politics differentiate between the self and the other.
Collective identification, as well as exclusion, is shown through the performance of religious ceremonies in which the likes of Laxman are prohibited
from participating. It enables and reifies their sense of self.

This works through othering. They are seen as "not us" and thereby
endanger "us". Such others threaten to take away from what "you"

have, as the legitimate subject of the nation, as the one who is the true recipient of national benefits.

(Ahmed 2000: 2)

The urban middle-class audience is very aware of these biases as it is part of their memories. Haksar turns this very process of othering through the use of emotions of disgust by employing subversive humour as a trope. There are several scenes concerned with the difference in the eating habits of the individuals from the migrant communities and those in the privileged positions. Whenever the upper-class, upper-caste people are shown to be eating or serving food, the music chosen is Indian Classical, and the movements are highly stylised and exaggerated. The women are shown dancing a classical dance form like Bharatnatyam or Kathak as they enter to serve food, eliciting laughter from the audience. The condescending and patronising bodies of these women are deconstructed through the use of humour and are also used to underscore the absurdity of the movements that exemplify the divide in the popular imagination.

Haksar's works are interventionist; they advocate the rights of the subaltern. At the same time, by highlighting and foregrounding the class-caste distinctions, they also repeat the norm. The discourse of the *Other* in the very act of its representation elucidates its category. Nevertheless, I see Haksar's works as enabling an interrogation of the accepted silence around this discrimination and thus can affectively evoke feelings like shame, guilt, empathy, and remorse amongst the audience.

Through her dramatisation of habits of thought, she is asking questions about the persecution faced by the internally displaced people who are living on the margins of the cities and who have been forced to migrate from a very unstable homeland replete with economic and physical dangers. In her productions, there is a conscious effort to stay away from the nauseating monotony of realism and an attempt to undo the hegemony of verbose theatrical traditions and conventional styles of expression. The emphasis is on the depiction of the *Other*, in their own voices, their own habitat, and their own body language onstage.

Notes

1 *Ucchaka* was performed in 2008 by the third-year National School of Drama students at Abhimanch, Delhi.
2 *Composition on Water* was performed at the Kochi Muziris Biennale in 2016 at Fort Kochi.
3 They began to leave in much greater numbers in the 1990s at a time of increased militancy, following persecution and threats by radical Islamists and militants.

4 Ebrahim Alkazi was an acclaimed theatre director and pedagogue who trained at RADA and, thereafter, became the director of the National School of Drama from 1962–1977.
5 Dhasal was a co-founder of the Dalit Panthers, a 1970s and 1980s anti-caste organisation inspired by the Black Panther movement in America. As a writer and activist, he was known to challenge dominant elitist discourses promoted by religion, tradition, and philosophy, focusing often on caste-based struggles.
6 Kristeva would argue that the abject content of Dhasal's work is "the jettisoned object, radically excluded, which draws me towards the place where meaning collapses" (11).

Works cited

Ahmed, Sara. "The Performativity of Disgust." *The Cultural Politics of Emotion*, NED—New ed., 2nd ed., Edinburgh UP, 2014, pp. 82–100.
———. *Strange Encounters: Embodied Others in Post-Coloniality*. Routledge, 2000.
Carlson, Marvin. *Speaking in Tongues: Languages at Play in the Theatre*. U of Michigan P, 2006.
Cixous, Hélène. "The Laugh of the Medusa." *New French Feminisms*, edited by Elaine Marks and Isabelle de Courtivron, Schocken, 1981, pp. 245–264.
Cox, Emma. *Performing Noncitizenship: Asylum Seekers in Australian Theatre, Film and Activism*. Anthem Press, 2015.
Gaikwad, Laxman. *The Branded*. Sahitya Akademi, 1999.
Jain, Indu. "Feminist Processes and Performance: Interventions in Anamika Haksar's Antar Yatra." *Theatre Research International*, vol. 42, no. 3, 2017, pp. 333–341.
———. Personal Interview with Anamika Haksar, Mumbai. Oct. 2016.
Kristeva, Julia. *Powers of Horror: An Essay on Abjection*. Columbia UP, 1982.
Lavender, Andy. *Performance in the Twenty-First Century: Theatres of Engagement*. Routledge, 2016.
Pavis, Patrice. "On Brecht's Notion of Gestus." *Languages of the Stage: Essays in the Semiology of the Theatre*. Translated by Susan Melrose. John Benjamin Publishing Company, 1982, pp. 90–104.
Said, Edward. *Representations of the Intellectual: The 1993 Reith Lectures*. Vintage, 1996.

9 Multilingual dramaturgy and staging relevant translations in Singapore

Alvin Eng Hui Lim

The terms "multicultural" and "multilingual" are often brandished as identity markers of Singapore and its population, but they tend to be articulated along racial-ethnic lines of Chinese, Malay, Indian, and Other (CMIO). This entrenched yet reductive plurality separates people into neat categories but fails to capture the complex intersections of identity, language, and everyday experience. As Brenda Yeoh explains, this "view of Singapore as a multiracial, multilingual, multicultural and multireligious society, potentially fissured along various fault-lines but held together by the nation-building framework" (2434) informs mainstream discourse surrounding Singapore's status as a cosmopolitan and global city (2442). Moreover, Charlene Rajendran argues that "Chinese, Malay and Indian cultures are widely performed as if these constructs remain unitary, and unchanged by social integration or proximity" (444). Singapore's model of multiculturalism "assumes and requires individuals to have a declared, unambiguous and unchanging ethnic identity" (Yeoh 2442). This attempt at multicultural integration becomes more pronounced and problematic as new waves of migration and transient foreign workers arrive in Singapore. Catherine Chua points out that "new waves of migration are more ethnically diverse and more multicultural than pervious [sic] migrations" (66). However, Singapore's postcolonial bilingual policy still "demands Singaporean children to acquire English as the first language (a colonial language), and one of the native languages (also known as Mother Tongue languages) as the second language" (66). This "native" language needs to be clarified, as the languages designated as such and as part of national education in schools are not always the actual first languages of Singaporean mothers and grandmothers. For example, children learn one of the official mother tongues:

> Mother Tongue Language (MTL) policy requires all students who are Singaporeans or Singapore Permanent Resident to study their respective official Mother Tongue Languages (MTLs): Chinese, Malay and

Tamil. A non-Tamil Indian may choose to take (a) Tamil, or (b) a non-Tamil Indian Language such as Bengali, Gujarati, Hindi, Punjabi or Urdu.

("General Information on Studying in Singapore")

This chapter examines the problematic definitions of identity and language in the context of theatre in Singapore. Designated as the lingua franca of modern Singapore, English enjoys a privileged status, though not without resistance and contradictions. Before Singapore gained its independence in 1965, English was already seen as an important language medium to forge a common identity (Lian 13).[1]

This translates to the Singapore stage where English as the performance language co-exists with other languages. The same CMIO language markers are often mapped onto theatres in Singapore, where theatre companies and speech and drama courses are likely to be grouped according to an official language.[2] It is against this backdrop that Singapore-based theatre companies often stage the struggle to embody language, whether consciously or not, and such stagings sometimes resist a simplistic performance of language. The issue and choice of performance language is especially pronounced when non-English productions normalise the use of English surtitles as a translation to accompany a "foreign" language on the Singapore stage.

To *speak* of translation in theatre is to be aware of the stakes involved in providing multiple languages for a stage performance—the "foreign" here constitutes a nexus of linguistic constructs and conventions, where a lingua franca (English) can also exist at the periphery. This chapter attends to the *relevance* of translation, which is by definition an attempt to provide access to audiences who do not understand a "foreign" language. A contradiction occurs when a supposed "native language" or "mother tongue" is performed onstage to audience members whose first and only language is English. This relevant translation extends to a working dramaturgy that shapes the performance of plays in multilingual Singapore. In looking at the term *relevant* as a dramaturgical strategy, this chapter attempts to find ways to discuss the relevance of theatre translation in a multilingual context.

I borrow the word *relevant* from Jacques Derrida (2001) because, as he points out, it connotes the continuity and relativity of language, predicating an audience that hears this language and for whom it is performed:

This word "relevant" carries in its body an ongoing process of translation . . . as a translative body, it endures or exhibits translation as the memory or stigmata of suffering [*passion*] or, hovering above it, as an aura or halo.

(Derrida 177)

In particular, the staging of bi- or multilingual translations on the Singapore stage demonstrates an "ongoing process of translation" that extends to the visual and kinetic (Lindsay 5). In that sense, and following Derrida, theatre makers and actors carry in their bodies and theatrically manifest "an ongoing process of translation". As a translative body, they "endure and exhibit translation as the memory or stigmata" of a mix of languages surrounding us. The slippages—from memory to body marks and back—describe how translation is embodied and disembodied through performance. They materialise in both voice production, sometimes in the shape and sound of the colloquial "Singlish",[3] and physical dissonance, where ethnicity suggested by skin colour sometimes distracts the spectator when he or she assumes that one language is associated with a certain skin. They also appear separately as text in the form of surtitles. In reality, these associations play a part in performance, where a mix of reception can occur when the same language as text and voice sound different to different audience members or when the surtitles do not quite match the spoken language.

Multilingual text and performance

Paul Rae argues that "performance-making is inherently a process of translation" (152), and this is highlighted in the work of the late Kuo Pao Kun. For example, Quah Sy Ren describes the multilingual play, *Mama Looking for a Cat*, written by Kuo Pao Kun, as a performance of "an irreconcilable gap between the older and younger generation" (90) where the languages of the older first- and second-generation migrant Singaporeans are forgotten by the younger generation. When the latter struggles to speak the languages of the former, the scenes collapse into miscommunication, gestural communication, and translation games that highlight the diminishing importance and prevalence of first-generation languages, such as Hokkien, Teochew, and Cantonese. Kuo's play highlights a fundamental societal change in its linguistic landscape at the time of its writing in the late 1980s—from the original "mother tongues" symbolically represented by the character Mama (or mother) to the English and Mandarin languages performed and written by Mama's children. Scenes in the play present the children's struggle to translate everyday English terms into Hokkien but are well-versed in the two official languages, Mandarin and English. In print, however, *Mama Looking for Her Cat* is only translated and written into English and Mandarin, which erases the subtleties of the play's multilingual translation. For example, Mama teaches her children to sing a Hokkien lullaby. The published text, however, does not render the Chinese characters into Hokkien but into Mandarin:

妈妈 让我先教你
们歌词：
"孩子乖乖睡，一
夜大一寸。
孩子妈妈疼，一
夜大一尺。
摇儿日落山，抱
儿**近近**看。
儿是我心肝，怕
他受风寒。" (In
Mandarin)

婴仔婴婴眠，
一暝大一寸。
婴仔婴婴惜，
一暝大一尺。
摇子日落山，
抱子**金金**看。
你是我心
肝，惊你受
风寒。(In
Hokkien)[4]

Mama Let me tell you the words
first:
Baby, baby, sleep
One night grow one inch.
Baby, baby, sleep,
One night grow one foot.
Minding baby till sun sets,
Cuddling baby **close** to me.
Baby, baby, you're my heart
Take care, take care, don't catch
cold. (In "Singlish")

When performing this text, then, any staging of this play must reflect the regression in competence of Hokkien as the children "grow up" in the later scenes. The actors learning to sing this song would have to translate the Mandarin text into Hokkien. More specifically, the Hokkien phrase written in Chinese characters, "金金" (Mandarin: *Jin*; Hokkien: *Kim Kim*) is difficult to translate into Mandarin or English. The two characters have been changed to "近近" (*Jin Jin*) in Mandarin, which in this context means to bring the child closer to the mother. Yet "金金" (*Jin Jin*) means gold with double emphasis. Nevertheless, both carry the meaning of looking closer and treating the child as preciously as one would treat gold (金). At one level, the published text repeats the simplification of Chinese characters (from the traditional script to the simplified script). At the corporeal level however, an actor may be at odds with the languages and must embody this, especially if the actor is unaware of the linguistic-cultural difference, as he or she learns it for performance. Preparing the actors to sing a faithful rendition of the song would require a Hokkien pronunciation of the characters. In the play, the children eventually learn to sing the lullaby as Mama would sing it. This scene, however, is not a demonstration of an authentic Hokkien song but anticipates the slow diminishing of Hokkien (and other languages) as English and Mandarin dominate the minority languages later in the play. Performing this play in a contemporary context would require a careful consideration of its dramaturgy of translation.

Having said that, should an ethnic Chinese actor mis-articulate the particular cadence of a vernacular Southern Chinese language (Hokkien) in this case, it could represent onstage both a departure of sounds from a supposed origin – i.e., a failure to capture the sound and the idiomatic expressions, as well as a demonstration of how languages mix and loan from other languages. Through the simple homophone *Jin* (both "close" and "gold"), one reads the text as if they are the same. This tongue, both familiar and alien, is a result of a translative migration—from the source language to the present context of language learning and writing in Singapore and of the deep adoption of Mandarin as *the* Chinese language. In effect, Kuo's *Mama* performs existing asymmetries of language and representational politics to generations of audience – i.e., as relevant translations that oscillate between the peculiar and the foreign, the familiar and the construct. The issue here is not whether one is faithful to an authentic language but to provide a performative expression of Singapore's changing society and its linguistic landscape. A phrase like *Jin* illustrates how language is veiled as it shifts from text to performance and vice versa.

In the following sections, I shall further explore the significance of relevant translation in relation to dramaturgy as languages are realised onstage. Moreover, the plays I explore in this chapter perform what Enoch Brater would call "linguistically based cultural migration", bilingual or trilingual plays that potentially invite multiple meanings and performances (131). In the context of Singapore, dramaturgy is a process "whereby something gains a practical shape or comes into a material form" (Kotte 206 quoted in Turner and Behrndt 32). This material form, however, lingers on like stigmata as a genealogical trace and symbol as sections of an audience cannot access the *other* language but acknowledge and mis-acknowledge its existence and meaning when it is spoken.

Translative dramaturgy: "star" or "new"

Collaborating with my partner, Faith Ng, to write a multilingual play about a complex relationship between a father (Julius Foo) and his adopted son (Andre Chong) allowed me to gain first-hand insights into how a Mandarin text would be performed alongside spoken Hokkien. We wrote and translated the play, *You Are My Needle, I Am Your Thread* (2015) into multiple languages: English, Mandarin, and the local variant of Hokkien. Our director, Chen Yingxuan, decided to include surtitles in the dramatised reading of the play, displaying the Mandarin text when the son speaks in English and the English text when the father speaks in Hokkien and Mandarin. In retrospect, we were able to witness the intricate shifts between the speaking lines and the text. This was made more complicated by the fact that Foo consulted a Taiwanese friend to learn the accurate pronunciation of the Hokkien text. During the rehearsal process, however, I pointed out that a Singaporean character would not follow the Taiwanese variant of Hokkien but the Singapore variant, which involved very subtle differences and loan words, especially from Bahasa Melayu. In the first scene, for example, Father tells audience members of Malay loan words:

> "Salah, 这不是滚水。水我 balu pu."
> ["Salah (wrong), this is not boiled water. I balu (just) boiled the water."]

Figure 9.1 You Are My Needle, I Am Your Thread; written by Alvin Lim and Faith Ng; (L to R) Andre Chong as George and Julius Foo as Pa. November 6, 2015. The Arts House, Singapore

Credit: Photo by Checkpoint Theatre/Jeff Low

"这会 senang 吗？Tolong 你帮我。"
["Is this senang (easy)? Can you tolong (please) help me?"]

(Ng 308)

This process informed our revisions, as Father reflects on how loan words from Bahasa Melayu have entered the vocabulary of the Singaporean variant, such as *salah, senang, balu,* and *tolong.* Thus, it was constructive to involve language learning in the performance, reinforcing the experience of audience members who may have very little understanding of Hokkien. When observing the audience members during the performance, I noticed that most of them frequently turned their heads to read the English surtitles (in parentheses earlier) when Father speaks in Hokkien. Hence, they could read the composite sentences that consist of two or three languages spoken in Singapore.

In one instance, the choice to transliterate Singapore to "星加坡" (Cantonese: Sing-gaa-po) both in the script and the surtitles was a deliberate attempt to draw a reader's attention to how Singapore was called by the Cantonese and overseas Chinese before independence. This can only be glimpsed at when the character "星" appears on screen and on the page, but when spoken, the two characters "新" (*Xin*) and "星" (*Sing*) sound similar. This name for Singapore harks back to Father's time frame as he recounts his arrival in Singapore. When Singapore gained independence from the British, the government made the choice to switch to the Chinese name, using "新" (*Xin*) in order to reflect a nation that is always new.

Saying Singapore in Cantonese—especially if it is not one's language, even though one speaks in English—is an example of what Derrida calls the "performative contradiction of enunciation" (1998: 3). He goes further to question what it means to have only one language, as is the case for many in the younger generation of Singaporeans who cannot speak their supposed 'mother tongue'. But here I am more interested in the act of language enunciation despite its performative contradiction. In that sense, to speak (similarly) of a sound (*Sing* or *Xin*) is to assert the fusion of identities. Singapore is after all not English but a translation of Singapura, a Romanised transliteration of its Sanskrit name (Lion City). A slight change of a character can performatively reflect the distinct break from our past, where this Cantonese version of Singapore's name is a little-known fact. Thus, most audience members would not be aware of it.

This language, along with other enunciations of "dialects", as they are commonly called, performs a trajectory of languages that Singaporeans speak across generations. Apart from the erasure of dialects as text, replaced by a hybrid of Mandarin and English surtitles, the staging of the play exemplified the impossibility of actors to embody fully and authentically a supposed pure language (as if that were a possibility). When juxtaposed with English and Mandarin, both spoken (dialogue) and written (surtitles), audience members became acutely aware of their respective statuses. Surtitling performs an act of juxtaposition and thus exemplifies the wide gap between languages. In another more recent production, a joint production with Singaporean and Macau actors brings us closer to the significance of the translative bodies juxtaposed to reflect how language migrates through performance.

Pissed Julie: three bodies and languages, two geographies

Pissed Julie (2018) is a collaboration between the Macau Arts Festival 2018 and the Singapore-based theatre company, Nine Years Theatre (NYT). As part of NYT's focus of translating Western plays into Mandarin, Nelson Chia (artistic director) directed, adapted, and translated August Strindberg's *Miss Julie*. It was performed by actors from Singapore and Macau in Mandarin and Cantonese with English and Chinese surtitles (including closed

captions for the hearing impaired). The collaboration enabled NYT to perform at the Macau Arts Festival and later in Singapore. Because I was not
well-versed in Cantonese, when I saw a performance in Singapore one evening in May 2018, I relied on the English and Mandarin surtitles to follow
the Cantonese dialogue.

The actors from Singapore spoke in Mandarin, whilst the actors from
Macau spoke in Cantonese. Chia added a twist to his direction by casting
three actors to play each character. Each actor provided a different shade
to the character through voice and body: Julie was played by Kate Leong
(Macau), Mia Chee, and Jean Toh (Singapore); Jean was played by Leong
Fan Kai (Macau), Hang Qian Chou, and Timothy Wan (Singapore); and
Christine was played by Flora Ho Chi Iao, Mandy Cheang (Macau), and
Neo Hai Bin (Singapore), who cross-dressed.

Reviews of the production focused on how it comments on social constructs and identity, reimagining the classic play with its staging and casting. By listening to Cantonese (as spoken in Macau) alongside standard
Mandarin, one becomes acutely aware of the performative and migratory
nature of language. This deliberate juxtaposition reveals the entrenchment
of language policy in the respective postcolonial cities, albeit with different
circumstances and success. On the one hand, the Mandarin that the Singaporean actors speak signals the mother tongue learning that begins at a
young age, a standard form of Mandarin that has been further honed by
NYT's own training programme designed to improve their actors' diction in
standard Mandarin. On the other hand, Macau's own colonial history saw
the former Portuguese colony face its own language issues. When the Portuguese parliament passed a law in late 1991 making Chinese an official language in Macau, thus sharing the same status as Portuguese, this was largely
understood as a political act in anticipation of the transfer of the sovereignty
of Macau from the Portuguese Republic to the People's Republic of China
in 1999 (Yee 57). The Chinese were concerned about "raising the official
status of the Chinese language" and promoting *Putonghua* (Mandarin) as
the official language as seen in other regions of China, such as Guangzhou
and Hong Kong.

The majority of people from Macau speak Cantonese despite 400 years of
Portuguese rule (Yee 56) and the juxtaposition of the Cantonese-speaking
actors from Macau with the Mandarin-speaking Singaporean actors foregrounded opposing yet not dissimilar language realities brought about
by the impact of language policy specific to a supposed singular Chinese
language. But what is the Chinese language? As the actors alternated,
languages shifted as well, and one was made to perceive how language
can profoundly shape oneself. The simple yet profound act of bringing
together two different groups of actors of "Chinese" ethnicity highlights

the over-simplification of identity and the monolingualism imposed by the other. As Derrida has it,

> the monolingualism imposed by the other operates by relying upon that foundation, here, through a sovereignty whose essence is always colonial, which tends, repressively and irrepressibly, to reduce language to the Other, that is to the hegemony of the homogenous.
>
> (1998: 39–40)

Instead of a one-size-fits-all multiculturalism, actors were placed in an ethical relation that revealed the limitations of language. It was telling that when the characters speak to each other in different languages—when the Cantonese-speaking Julie talks to the Mandarin-speaking Jean—they pretended to understand each other. Perhaps they did understand each other, but it was not certain in the context of the play, since they were not speaking the same (spoken) language. Instead, they relied on a *relevant translation*, a desire to communicate despite the monolingualism imposed by the sovereign other. Suspending a realistic dialogue, actors from two geographies and descendants of Chinese migrants burdened by the languages they possess presented the opposing trajectories of Chinese persons speaking their respective tongues. Yet they shared the same stage, persisting in performing a translation of a Western play.

This observation leads me to think about the importance of multilingual dramaturgy. Deferring in body and language, multilingual dramaturgy is a perceptive way to consider the performance of language alongside the bodies of performers who embody all the contradictions of identity. In the case of *Pissed Julie*, the juxtaposition shows a language heterogeneity that goes beyond superficial language speaking, a language that "exists asymmetrically, always for the *other*, from the other, kept by the other" (Derrida 40). This created a compact bilingual soundscape in which one was constantly hearing things twice over. In that sense, it cannot be assumed that language is a given or that an actor possesses all the corporeal aspects of a singular language: its accents, tones, inflections, and rhythms. Chia's direction highlights how (Chinese) bodies migrate with languages or rather how languages migrate in spite of the bodies. In the context of a touring production, they gathered to exhibit two or more "Chinese" bodies, each with a language to perform and embody. Thus, for the actors, the Mandarin is not a mother tongue, not a maternal speech as Derrida would say. Co-opted as the "mother tongue" of Chinese Singaporeans, it persists as another colonial act enshrined by the state's ongoing rhetoric that Singapore possesses specific official languages for each ethnicity. The production of *Pissed Julie* unwittingly reveals all the complexities of identity formation.

Theatre situated in a place like Singapore is what Derrida calls "a place of fantasy . . . at an ungraspable distance" (1998: 42). The successive campaigns to "Speak Good Mandarin" that the Singapore government organises insist on a "model of good speech and good writing" and thus "represented the language of the master" (42). But we know from theatre all the complexities that language embodiment present. It is a place to grasp distances. The Cantonese is, in the context of theatre, a language of the Other for local audiences who do not understand Cantonese and performing it provides an opportunity to imagine a minority language, a dialect in Singapore, as another source of emotional connection, characterisation, or simply another linguistic reality for its own majority.

Conclusion

To stage multilingual plays is to embody all the difficulties and limitations of cultural representation. It is often too straightforward to claim languages as distinct units. It is also important to recognise how languages develop or when a pidgin language can develop or migrate into creole through language acquisition across a generation or more (Anderson and Shirai 527–528). In terms of dramaturgy, one must also be aware of the diversity of audiences. They may be of different language competencies in spite of, or rather because of, living in a multilingual society. A multilingual society does not necessarily mean a linguistically porous community, where languages are spoken and understood interchangeably. To provide English surtitles would be an important step to provide access, but doing so would also introduce the question of attention—how does one decide which performance to focus on? As English surtitles are shown as part of a multilingual performance, they force those who do not understand the language onstage to pay more attention to the text. In that respect, they shift their gaze from the speaking body to the mediated text and back. Instead of performing language as a given identity or a sense of linguistic purity, translation contributes to the critical dramaturgy required to question language at the most personal and emotional level of self. Above all, multilingual dramaturgy must treat languages as one's intimate possession to articulate from within one's identity. After all, when we travel and speak, we face the other who senses us.

Notes

1 In the interest of forging a common community in the impending federation, in 1950, the Barnes Report recommended the use of only Malay or English in schools. In response to the consternation of the Chinese community that the recommendation would lead to the demise of Chinese language and culture, the government commissioned the Fenn-Wu Report in 1951. The authors took the

view that the educational system of co-existing English and vernacular languages preceded the concept of a "Malayan" nation, believing that a Malayan community could not be created by fiat as implied in the Barnes Report (Hill and Lian, 73–74). They accordingly counter-proposed that English and vernacular education be given equal treatment (Lian 14).

2　The People's Association, for example, a statutory board established to "promote racial harmony and social cohesion in Singapore" since 1 July 1960 (People's Association, www.pa.gov.sg/about-us), lists on its "onePA" website speech and drama courses in Chinese, English, Malay, and Tamil, respectively. *See* www.onepa.sg/cat/speech-and-drama.

3　In reference to the English-based Creole spoken language, often mixing with other vernacular languages found in Singapore.

4　I have rendered this into traditional script and Taiwanese Hokkien, as this song is still commonly known in Taiwan.

Works cited

Anderson, R. W., and Yasuhiro Shirai. *Handbook of Second Language Acquisition*. Academic Press Inc., 1996.

Brater, Enoch. "Beckett, 'Thou Art Translated'." *Theatre Translation in Performance*, edited by Silvia Bigliazzi, Peter Kofler, and Paola Ambrosi, Routledge, 2013, pp. 130–139.

Chua, Catherine S. K. "A New Model of Bilingualism for Singapore: Multilingualism in the Twenty-First Century." *Minority Languages and Multilingual Education: Bridging the Local and the Global*, edited by Durk Gorter, Victoria Zenotz, and Jasone Cenoz, Springer, 2013, pp. 65–84.

Derrida, Jacques. *Monolingualism of the Other or The Prosthesis of Origin*. Translated by Patrick Mensah, Stanford UP, 1998.

———. "What Is a Relevant Translation?" *Critical Inquiry*, vol. 27, 2001, pp. 174–200.

"GENERAL INFORMATION ON STUDYING IN SINGAPORE." *Ministry of Education Singapore*, www.moe.gov.sg/admissions/returning-singaporeans/general-information-on-studying-in-singapore. Accessed 1 June 2018.

Hill, Michael, and Kwen Fee Lian. *The Politics of Nation Building and Citizenship in Singapore*. Routledge, 1995.

Kotte, Andreas. *Theaterwissenschaft*. Bohlau, 2005.

Kuo, Pao Kun. "寻找小猫的妈妈 [Mama Looking for Her Cat]." *The Complete Works of Kuo Pao Kun: Volume Two*, edited by Quah Sy Ren and Pan Zhenglei, The Theatre Practice and Global Publishing, 2012, pp. 169–181.

———. "Mama Looking for Her Cat." *The Complete Works of Kuo Pao Kun: Volume Four*, edited by C. J. W.-L. Wee, The Theatre Practice and Global Publishing, 2012, pp. 81–97.

Lian, Kwen Fee. *Multiculturalism, Migration, and the Politics of Identity in Singapore*, Springer Science+Business Media, 2016.

Lindsay, Jennifer. "Translation and/of/in Performance: New Connections." *Between Tongues: Translation and/of/in Performance in Asia*, edited by Jennifer Lindsay, NUS Press, 2006, pp. 1–32.

Ng, Faith (with Alvin Lim). "You Are My Needle, I Am Your Thread." *Faith Ng: Plays Volume One*, edited by Lucas Ho, Checkpoint Theatre, 2016, pp. 306–353.

Quay Sy Ren. "Performing Multilingualism in Singapore." *Between Tongues: Translation and/of/in Performance in Asia*, edited by Jennifer Lindsay, NUS Press, 2006, pp. 88–103.

Rae, Paul. "In Tongues: Translation, Embodiment, Performance." *Translation in Asia: Theories, Practices, Histories*, edited by Ronit Ricci and Jan van der Putten, St Jerome Publishing, 2011, pp. 152–166.

Rajendran, Charlene. "Multicultural Play as 'Open Culture' in 'Safe Precincts': Making Space for Difference in Youth Theatre." *Research in Drama Education: The Journal of Applied Theatre and Performance*, vol. 21, no. 4, 2016, pp. 443–458. doi:10.1080/13569783.2016.1220243.

Turner, Cathy, and Synne K. Behrndt. *Dramaturgy and Performance*, Palgrave Macmillan, 2008.

Yee, Albert H. *Macau in Transition: From Colony to Autonomous Region*, Palgrave Macmillan, 2001.

Yeoh, Brenda S. A. "Cosmopolitanism and Its Exclusions in Singapore." *Urban Studies*, vol. 41, no. 12, 2004, pp. 2431–2445.

Part III

On dramaturgy of globalised, transnational, and cosmopolitan encounters

10 I am a war, my voice is a weapon

Language as identity in monodramas by South African youth

Judith Rudakoff

Over the last decade, I have been fortunate to work within communities that are geographically distant from my home base of Toronto, Canada, and culturally distinct from my own ethnicity and experience. In trying to forge ways to work dramaturgically in a diversity of communities, often without benefit of shared language or iconography, my aim has been to create and evolve a set of dramaturgical tools that would work transculturally to inspire creativity. This led me first to work with *The Four Elements* (Rudakoff 2003), exploring the many different perceptions of air, earth, water, and fire and their interrelationships, given the specifics of time and place and of the landscape and climate within which we were working. But I also wanted a less intellectual way of working with groups, where a prompt could be offered quickly, and a creative response could come without the need to "think it through". I began to experiment with how the idiosyncratic and unpredictable photographs taken with a Russian LOMO camera (or lomographs) could be used as creative tools. Lomographs tend to be evocative rather than documentary. These are not snapshots that encapsulate a moment for subsequent examination or analysis. They give movement shape and shape movement. Images can appear diffused and distorted or emanate from an unexpected or warped perspective. Conversely, images can intensify and offer a pointed focus on normally insignificant details. Colours, particularly if cross-processed from slide film to colour print, are highly saturated. The LOMO Kompakt recognises the ordinary minutiae of daily life in odd ways. Finally, you don't really look *at* a Lomograph but *into* it.

When I use the set of 90 laminated image cards drawn from my LOMO photographs (which I call *Lomograms*) as prompts whilst dramaturging creative work, they elicit strong immediate responses, often from people who are not comfortable with or accustomed to expressing themselves in any artistic medium, written or performative. By distorting reality, Lomograms provide a visual springboard for the imagination as well as de-emphasising the cultural context for objects or locations (Rudakoff 2014).

These and other artistic provocations that are not dependent on a shared understanding of language, context, or community have proven time and again that authentic creative practice driven by transcultural dramaturgy methods is rooted in the exploration and expression of the self and the relationship to home. The related challenge—how and where to root the self and/or to identify home—is one grappled with by displaced, exiled, colonised, Othered, or disenfranchised people the world over. Developing transcultural dramaturgy methods and applying them has helped me to understand more about this fraught relationship between personal and cultural identity.

As I wrote in the introduction to *Dramaturging Personal Narratives: Who Am I and Where Is Here?*,

> the developmental dramaturgy I practice often begins with an investigation into how people perceive self, home, and homeland and how they inter-relate these concepts. My dramaturgical methods involve prompting personal narratives, sometimes provoking those narratives through a variety of pretexts and constructed projects. I try to ensure that all participants find ways and means of expressing their histories and experiences that are unique to their lives, yet are accessible and understandable to as far-reaching and diverse an audience or readership as possible. No matter what their socio-economic or political status, for many participants the voicing or enacting of personal narratives (and the realization that these individual stories can be universally affective) is empowering. As well, recognizing similarity within difference has been illuminating for both contributors and viewers.
>
> (Rudakoff 2014: 3)

Dramaturgical tools in practice

As an invited artist/scholar in residence at the University of Cape Town (UCT), South Africa, in August 2016, I initiated, dramaturged, and directed a site-specific cycle of short, original, thematically linked monodramas titled *The Ashley Plays: Blood and Water* over an intensive two-week period.

These monodramas, focusing on home as a contested site, questioning citizenship, and challenging the balance of power, were created and subsequently performed at locations throughout the university's Hiddingh Campus by the 16 members of the UCT 2016 third year Conservatory Acting programme. These actors, none of whom had written for live performance before, used their home languages as well as English to translate their strongly felt fears, anger, pride, and individual identity into dramatic characters and theatrical narratives. My perspective is that of a practising dramaturg, and, therefore, this chapter will reflect the nature of my engagement with the work, which is practical and documentative rather than theoretical.

Each participant chose a site somewhere on campus and that location was incorporated in an integral way to provide a dramatic context for their performance. No artificial sound, light, costumes, or props were permitted. On the performance day, four audience pods of approximately 30 spectators were led through the 16 sites on 4 different routes, viewing the plays in different sequence.

These performer/writer participants, who included freeborns (born in South Africa after the fall of apartheid) as well as a small number of international students, identified their heritage as Xhosa, Zulu, Sesotho, Afrikaaner, white European, South Asian/Cape Malay, Danish, and Chilean/American, with a large proportion of them also identifying as mixed race with white European/black African ancestry, known in South Africa as Coloured. Rather than English, the first language of many of the participants included Afrikaans, isiXhosa, isiZulu, Sotho, Hindi, Spanish, and Danish, as well as hybrid languages and neighbourhood-specific versions and dialects. The languages spoken in the plays contained indicators of their creators' migration from ancestral/family homes to student/temporary homes. (Cape Town, it should be noted, has 11 primary languages: English, Afrikaans, the Nguni languages (isiZula, isiXhosa, isiNdebele, isiSwati), the Sothoi-Tswana languages (Sesotho sa Leboa, Sesotho, Setswana), Xitsonga, and Tshivenda. The anticipated audience of peers, family, friends, and general public were projected to speak and understand at least one of the languages used. This meant that at any given moment during the performance cycle, different audience members might or might not understand either the spoken text or references implied by the particular use of words or expressions. This mirrored the daily Cape Town experience and reflected the hierarchy of certain shared languages (English, for example, was the most widely understood language).

Geoffrey Hyland, associate professor and head of the Drama Department at UCT, commented,

> I teach a diverse body of actors and theatre-makers and often I will be presented with a performance piece where I don't understand the words because they are in one of the eleven languages or related dialects that are spoken in and around Cape Town. And I encourage that incorporation of home languages; it's a critical part of teaching performance in a multicultural society.
>
> (Hyland)

One of the international participants, Peter Wiisbye, had lived in South Africa for three years at the time of the project. He offered this perspective on the use of multiple languages in the cycle:

> Despite any language barrier that I experienced as a Danish person in South Africa, the use of multiple languages in *The Ashley Plays* made the performances much stronger. I found it incredibly powerful to hear my classmates perform in their native language. It drew in the spectators in a way that I have not seen before, whilst making the performances much more personal, private and intimate.
>
> (Wiisbye)

The goal of this project was to have each participant generate and develop a monodrama of under five minutes, expressed through the voice of a character named Ashley, or about Ashley, in the language of their choice.[1] Like Hyland, during the two-week work period, I often found myself not understanding the full text of the work being developed. I saw this not as a problem but as an opportunity to give the creators agency. We would discuss the content of the narrative being evolved, but they had control over *how* the stories were being transmitted. Form reflected cultural background and styles of storytelling.

This central Ashley character was to be created independently by each participant, initiated by some of the provocative characteristics chosen by the group as inspiration. Whilst participants could not contradict any aspect of the general profile, each Ashley was to be different, inspired by the writer-performer's own life, informed by their cultural influences, and, for most, reflecting the experience of moving from a village, town, or small city to a major cosmopolitan centre. The Ashley creation process offered participants the opportunity to express the personal and, if necessary, to do so from within a protective frame. Speaking *as* Ashley has proven to be liberating for participants in the many iterations of *The Ashley Plays* that I have dramaturged over the past 15 years.[2] Additionally, a theme was introduced: what is home to you? Is home a place of safety or of danger? Is home where you belong? Reflecting on the nature of home gave participants the opportunity to express their relationship to both their ancestral home and their current temporary home. The language and dialects spoken in the plays were indicators of the cultural identity of each Ashley, at times blending a traditional identity with an assumed identity or the public personae of these migrants.

To begin the writing process, I introduced the Four Elements and asked the participants to create "Image Flash" writing inspired by one of the elements. The Image Flash method asks participants to focus on a remembered event, an element, or a visual cue (like a Lomogram) and quickly write a list of succinct images, each beginning with the words "There are stories about" (TASA). By providing a catalogue of images, this text-generating exercise results in a large number of cues without expanding on the story of each specific image. The goal is for the Image Flash list to act as a creative menu for later use when the image is ready to be mined and integrated into a work. Because the emphasis in this exercise is on chronicling rather than editing and revising, even participants who did not identify as writers found themselves exceeding their personal expectations by generating evocative text fragments. Some participants wrote Image Flash exercises in the voice of their Ashley character and later incorporated the images or stories inspired by the exercise into their individual play. Others used the TASAs verbatim. For example, Wynand Ferreira, who is white and speaks Afrikaans, began and ended his play with a TASA list of the names of murdered white South African farmers from his home near Oudtshoorn in the arid Little Karoo area of the Western Cape. His play explored the emotional tie to the land that he and his white ancestors have and grappled with his conflicted feelings about land ownership rights.

Next in the writing process, I introduced the Lomogram image cards, and the participants continued writing either more "Image Flash" exercises or monologues inspired by this visual challenge.

These writing exercises were then developed into short narrative-driven monodramas within the parameters of the Ashley project.

The plays

Xhosa participant Mandla Mpanjukelwa[3] created a play about an Ashley character who was prepared to die for the right to maintain ownership of his land when the Freedom Charter of 1955 was being violated by government forces. Looking back at that struggle, Mpanjukelwa's Ashley was portrayed as a renegade and a fugitive. When faced with police and military intervention, this Ashley is warned to run, as Nelson Mandela ran, after the newly adopted Freedom Charter was almost immediately denounced as an act of treason and became an underground manifesto.

Mpanjukelwa grew up in Mitchell's Plain, a township that sits just outside of the city of Cape Town, which he characterises as part of the "crime and gang-infested Cape Flats area." (Mpanjukelwa 2017).[4]

He described his relationship to his ancestral home in the Eastern Cape as follows: "I am a culmination of what has come before me, my roots lay deep in the red soil of the Eastern Cape region, where my Xhosa-populated villages can be found, in Indwe" (Mpanjukelwa 2017).

Mpanjukelwa spoke in both English and his first language, isiXhosa, in his play. He presented his piece in a basement dressing room, surrounded by mirrors. Mpanjukelwa used the mirrors in his performance, sometimes directing text to his own reflection and other times turning from the mirrors, directly addressing the audience, and letting them see themselves reflected as he spoke. To make Ashley's identity more Xhosa, Mpanjukelwa changed the name to the more familiar-sounding "Asheni."

Here is an excerpt from his play:

> There are stories about Asheni.
> There are stories about Asheni's disappearance.
> *kuthethwa ngomntwana owaduka lingekatshoni ilanga.* [*Translation: I speak of a child that set before sunset.*][5]
> There are stories about his recovery, only nobody knows these stories;
> *Ngamabali okuvaleleka* [*Translation: These are stories of entrapment*],
> Trapped.
> Stories where light mirrors the dark and, as they have it, well . . .
> *Babemfanisa nobumnyama, bumnyama obabungenguye nxeba lomnt' o-ntsundu* [*Translation: They never had it, they spoke about Asheni*].
> They saw him as blackness, darkness! That is what blacks were diminished to.
> There are stories about Asheni.
> *Nabo besiza emvakwakho, baleka, baleka* [*Translation: They are coming after you, run, run!*]
> Asheni stop, breathe, listen.
> Hush little child.
> *Thu' ulalele.* [*Translation: Hush and listen*]
> While I try to mend these bridges, bridges of smoke, tear-gas, blue lights shining in my eyes.
> I can't see, there is no future.
> Tonight they are taking Asheni away.

By incorporating his first language, Mpanjukelwa blurred the lines between home and adopted home. He remembered the town of Indwe, his ancestral home.[6] He spoke truths and expressed beliefs from the self, for the self, and to the outside audience. By including text that not all the spectators would understand, Mpanjukelwa privileged the isiXhosa speakers, in a sense returning power to them in both the present place and in the historical situation where power was not in their hands.

Another play in the cycle was created by Luke Buys.[7] In an attempt to reclaim identity and contextualise heritage, Buys's Ashley was a man of mixed race or "Coloured." Buys reflected on the use of the term "Coloured" in South Africa (Figure 10.1):

Figure 10.1 Mandla Mpanjukwela in *The Ashley Plays: Blood and Water*, University of Cape Town, South Africa, August 12, 2016

Photo Credit: Rob Keith

It's a term [that was] used by the apartheid government to divide and conquer the indigenous peoples of South Africa. Hence, this term now still exists but is attached to a massive stereotype of "Coloured" people. For example, all Coloured people are gangsters, they [are] uncontrollably violent, they don't have respect for women.

(Buys)

In terms of using different languages in his Ashley play, Buys explained that context dictated choice. He wrote,

I cannot be the way I am at UCT Mowbray [the neighbourhood where student residences are located] compared to being back home in Mitchell's Plain. I would most probably die. So language plays a role in both setting a mode for example in the hood. You show no fear, make yourself big, be hard like stone and don't let them see your emotions. So the language, the words, is just the last part to this process.

(Buys)

Buys characterised his use of language in his Ashley play thusly:

> [The play] explores my personal views of life, religion, God and every-thing in-between. The language is predominantly Afrikaaps, a Cape slang spoken by people from the Cape Flats. However, Afrikaaps has often been misinterpreted with the inherently violent Sabela Taal, a uniquely coded language spoken by gangsters predominantly in the Western Cape, Cape Flats. Over the years the mixture of Afrikaaps and the Sabela Taal have become so deeply intertwined to an extent where many words have been adapted to Afrikaaps, although they may not share the same meaning in essence.
>
> (Buys)

This specific use of language locates the play and the character as he migrates from the familiarity of home to the challenging environment of the Cape Flats. It also makes portions of the text inaccessible to audiences who are not from the Cape Flats. By identifying language with location, Buys is working within the parameters of the dramaturgy of migration.

Before settling and living for several generations in Mitchell's Plain, Buys's family first lived in Cape Town's District Six, a city neighbourhood that was entirely dismantled when the South African government imple-mented a contentious and racist policy of forced removals of mixed-race inhabitants in the 1960s, re-settling them outside the city in townships.[8]

What follows is an excerpt from Buys's multi-layered, densely con-structed play, which was performed outdoors in front of the locked door to a room called the Playroom where the UCT theatre students regularly rehearsed and performed—their "home" on campus. In this Ashley play, the Playroom became privileged territory. The play began with Buys bang-ing on the locked door, asking and then demanding to be given leave to enter, but to no avail. He then turned and faced the assembled audience and addressed them directly, speaking his text as a rhythmic spoken-word exhor-tation. At times, the speaker was Ashley, and at other times, the speaker broke the fourth wall and addressed both the audience and Ashley as a nar-rator. The Playroom also took on different settings, from township com-munity home to individual home, always boundaried and always requiring special permission to enter/belong.

Buys's contextual explanations are included in **bold**.[9] Where literal trans-lation is possible, and where Buys has *chosen* to translate the words into English, the text is included in *italic*. Some sections remain untranslated, so the reader, like the audience, is not given access to all the spoken language or all the specific details of the play text (Figure 10.2).

Figure 10.2 Luke Buys in *The Ashley Plays: Blood and Water*, University of Cape Town, South Africa, August 12, 2016

Photo Credit: Rob Keith

There are stories about red painted floors turning streets into rivers of blood.

This refers to dead bodies of young men, women and children found in the streets every single day. Bloodstains on the ground long after the body has been removed.

There are stories that will never be told, that happened in the Playroom.

This comments on how communities live in fear of gangsters, they are all aware who the killers are but wouldn't dare to tell the police because of the risk of being killed, or losing a family member.

There are stories about Ashley.
There are stories about who Ashley is.
There are stories about home.

"Home" refers to a feeling of absolute comfort and ease in the body along with a peace of mind. A feeling of being safe.

Ek trap op die gronde van my voorvaarders en voormoeders met vooregte sone regte.
Wie is jy ?
Ek is die egte ? [Translation: I walk on the ground of my forefathers and foremothers with privileges but no rights. Who are you? I am the original.]

This translates into questions about identity, what it is to be Coloured in contemporary society. Who are my ancestors, where do I fit in into modern society? What is my history?

Displaced in a kingdom with no name, labelled by birth and born into shame.

Coloured people are constantly having to prove their worth as it is conceived that they do not own a history. It is often believed Coloured people were created by white Dutch settlers who slept with the black women and produced Coloureds. No real history, just a combination of the black and white. Also, challenging the stereotype that all Coloureds are gangsters, drug lords and inherently violent.

Ashley, can you explain?
Why I'm labelled by birth and born into shame.
Strangers?

Spiritual reference questioning God: why he would allow this to happen. He knows the future. Did he not see this coming? I want answers. I am born in South Africa my ancestors are the Khoisan [First People] and yet I find myself not able to belong. I have become a stranger in my own land.

As I fight against the grain,
Tirelessly I toil in the soil,
Desperately, searching for my roots.
Uprooted from The Six,
I am diluted,
Or better known as mixed.

I fight against the stereotypes, misconceived perceptions of Coloureds, and whilst in the midst of all this, I still search for my roots. "Uprooted from The Six" refers to the forced removals of people of colour who were violently evicted and stripped of their dignity. They were then placed in what is now known as the Cape Flats.

There are stories about blood in and blood out. This is my initiation known as the out-casted.

> **Growing up in the Flats, at a young age one will be tested to be recruited to work for the gangs. This process is a blood bond that brings you in and a blood bond that takes you out. When one wants to leave it could only be done by forfeiting your blood: death. In clear terms, there is no way out. Out-casted refers to you no longer owning an identity: you're just another number.**

Supreme Kingdoms built upon the blood of my brothers and tears of my mothers. Gone is a nation.

> **Talking about the gang leaders, drug lords and the elites who supply them with weapons. They live lavish lifestyles, cars, money, mansions, whilst the young foot soldiers die in the streets every day and they live long healthy lives.**

Ma Ek staan nog altyd Kapadien vi enige nomme wat wil maats, pangela hulle sal chise met on the battlefield, slowly lost in translation.

> **I am proud to be Coloured but not proud about what it is to be Coloured in contemporary society. We have become heartless, cold and driven by greed. How did we fall so low and is there any chance of redemption? We are no longer understood.**

To demonstrate the specificity of language and its ties to place and culture, I asked a white South African Afrikaans-speaking colleague to offer her translation of the non-English Afrikaans sections of Buys's play and she could not fully do so. For example,

> I suspect the word "*kapadien*" is of Arabic origin (the Cape Malay influence) and has probably been incorporated into the Cape Coloured / gangster slang. This slang is almost like another language all of its own . . . and very effectively excludes people who are not part of the culture!
>
> (Naudé)

Conclusion

These samples from *The Ashley Plays: Blood and Water* and the examination of how language was representative of identity and location (as well as an important element of the transmission of meaning in the component monodramas) offer examples of how this simple yet complex project was able to elicit compelling and deeply personal dramatic responses. Free-dom of expression became part of the goal of the presentation, as in some cases, the audience's understanding and interpretation was reliant solely on visual cues and physical vocabulary. By incorporating material in their home language, performed to audiences who often only understood some of the spoken text, these plays took on additional meaning: the expression of individual voice in a language chosen by the writer/performer was activ-ism in action. In what might be seen as a war zone, where daily battles are fought to establish and maintain cultural identity, voice expressed through language is a powerful weapon.

Notes

1 When I first developed *The Ashley Plays*, I chose the name Ashley for this central character for several reasons: the name is non-gender-specific; it is easy to pro-nounce in many languages, and it has equivalents in many cultures. In India, the name was changed to Ashok. In the Canadian High Arctic, in Nunavut, the name was changed to Ashevok.
2 For discussion and examples, see Judith Rudakoff, *Dramaturging Personal Nar-ratives: Who Am I and Where Is Here?* Intellect Press, 2014.
3 Mandla Mpanjukelwa holds a BA in theatre and performance from UCT, specialis-ing in acting.
4 This citation is from an unpublished biography submitted by Mandla Mpanjukelwa.
5 The text in brackets is the English translation of the isiXhosa text and was not spoken in performance.
6 In Xhosa culture, home is where your umbilical cord is buried.
7 Born and raised in Cape Town, Luke Buys graduated from the UCT with a BA diploma in theatre and performance, specializing in acting.
8 On February 11, 1966, the apartheid government declared Cape Town's District Six a whites-only area under the Group Areas Act of 1950. From 1968, over 60,000 of its inhabitants were forcibly removed to the Cape Flats over 25 kilo-meters away. Except for the local houses of worship, the buildings were system-atically bulldozed throughout the 1970s and by 1982, almost all evidence of the district had been destroyed. (www.saha.org.za/news/2010/February/district_six_recalling_the_forced_removals.htm)
9 I have not edited Buys context statements to maintain authenticity of voice.

Works cited

Buys, Luke. 26 Oct. 2017. Facebook Messenger.
Collison, Lee-Shay. "A Guide to Languages Spoken in South Africa." *Culture Trip*, 29 Sept. 2016, https://theculturetrip.com/africa/south-africa/articles/a-guide-to-languages-spoken-in-south-africa/.
Hyland, Geoffrey. Email to the Author. 28 Mar. 2018.
Mpanjukelwa, Mandla. 11 May 2017. Facebook Messenger.
Naudé, Natanja. Email to the Author. 13 Oct. 2017.

Rudakoff, Judith. "Forging New Dramaturgy Tools: Lomogram Image Cards." *Theatre Topics*, Fall 2014, pp. 261–267.

———. "The Four Elements: New Models for a Subversive Dramaturgy." *Theatre Topics*, Mar. 2003, pp. 143–153

South African History Archive. "District Six: Recalling the Forced Removals." *South African History Archive*, 11 Feb. 2010, www.saha.org.za/news/2010/February/district_six_recalling_the_forced_removals.htm.

Wiisbye, Peter. Email to the Author. 16 Feb. 2018.

11 From Chinese local history to another memory

An interview with Folk Memory Project on their workshop with African refugees

Sun Weiwei

Preface

Folk Memory Project (FMP) is an ongoing artistic/social project organised by Caochangdi Workstation (CCD) in 2010 in Beijing, China. CCD was founded by acclaimed filmmaker Wu Wenguang and choreographer Wen Hui in Beijing in 2005. It is based in Wu's film studio and in Wen's Living Dance Studio, a renowned independent platform for young artists in China to create their own work. The underlying aim of FMP is to unearth the personal memories of the victims of the 1959–1961 "Great Chinese Famine" (三年大饥荒) and to create an archive of these otherwise-unrecorded folk memories. This famine functionally erased the lives of 36 million people—people whose lives and memories were never officially documented by the Chinese government. Drought, poor weather, and the policies of Mao Zedong contributed to the widespread famine, though the relative weights of each of these contributors are widely disputed.

By 2018, FMP had produced hundreds of text reports, 54 documentary films, and 8 dance/theatre performances surrounding the newly uncovered folk memories. Over 200 artists and students participated in this project, going to 190 villages in 22 provinces and interviewing more than 1,400 villagers from the ages of 60 to 100. This project primarily focused on the idea of "oral memory" and its intrinsic use of language.

Although FMP doesn't have a multicultural background, film and theatre festivals and art residencies outside of China have sought out its work. Moreover, the principal artists Wu Wenguang and Zhang Mengqi have used their strategies of collecting "oral memory" in a variety of global contexts. For instance, in 2017, the artists conducted a workshop in Cagliari, Italy, with more than 20 male refugees aged 17 to 32 from over ten countries in Africa. The workshop was organised by Boundary·Art and hosted by

Carovana S.M.A., which aims to foster collaboration between local communities and artists from different backgrounds and nationalities—in this case, the African refugees in Italy. By recording and performing the refugees' personal memories of their homeland and subsequent exile, Wu and Zhang attempted to create a therapeutic journey to constructively release the migrants' emotional pain and to encourage new relationships between participants. The project consisted of two sections: a physical workshop in June that lasted for more than two weeks and a one-week documentary film workshop in November. At the end of the first workshop, 19 African refugees, together with a 16-year-old female Ukrainian migrant, performed a collective theatre piece, *African Memory: Crossing* at Theatre Massimo.

This interview builds on the role of language in FMP. In discussing *African Memory: Crossing*, it asks how these artists employ the artistic methodologies they developed in China to work in an international context and how they arrange the diverse languages to reflect the personal memories of the refugees.

Sun Weiwei: As Hans-Thies Lehmann notes in his book *Postdramatic Theatre*, "the new theatre text is to a large extent a 'no longer dramatic' theatre text" (17). What role does language play in Folk Memory Project? Is the language dramatic or just a dramaturgical material?

Wu Wenguang: In my opinion, the recordings of people's memories in our works are dramatic because memories are often stories, sometimes fictions. Nevertheless, although people's memories are the starting point and the essential element of our works, it is evident that the core aesthetic of our eight performances is not narrative. In our shows, the recordings are more like separated texts composing a socio-symbolic scene rather than a drama. I think this is the dominant difference in comparing the language of our works to a "conventional" drama. Take our latest theatre work, *Reading Hunger*, as an example. Apart from the old people talking on the screen, the entire performance by the young performers is wordless. They use only their bodies to represent a connection or a reaction to the memories of the elderly. The work is divided into several sections (memorise, hunger, eat, pain, death, sigh, etc.) So in the "eat" part, the elders recall what they ate during the famine, such as bark, grassroots, leaves, bran. And then the performers onstage start to tremble, an action that can last from three to five minutes. Therefore, although the elders' words are relatively dramatic, they don't provoke a coherent narration but only function as a kind of "trigger" to activate the reactions of the young people. In short, I think the verbal communication in our theatre can be regarded as dramaturgical material but not narration.

Sun Weiwei: During the workshop with the African refugees, how did you communicate? Did you use different languages?

Wu Wenguang: Indeed, the difficulty in communicating with the African refugees was mainly due to language. Most of them speak only French or their native language, and we could hardly understand their English because of their accents. So we had a translator, the organiser of the Boundary·Art project, an Italian choreographer, who helped the refugees translate their words into English. But as English was not the original language for any of us, it was impossible to get the "real" words from each other. To introduce our work, we did a special lecture performance and a physical workshop for the refugees. During the screening of some videos of the elders talking about the famine, Mengqi was doing physical performances. Since this method relies mainly on images and movements, it quickly gained the refugees' interest so that when we asked who want to join this workshop, 25 people raised their hands! Our methodology drew thereafter on our two core elements, oral memory and physical connection.

The primary connection between FMP and the refugees is the personal memory of suffering, as these young Africans all had experiences of escaping death similar to those of the old people in China. So we began the workshop in a similar way as in the works of FMP: we asked the participants to tell their personal histories. The theme of the first workshop was "Across the Memory". We asked them to talk about how they travelled by boat, crossing the border, returning to their hometowns, etc. Some said it was the first time they talked about these memories publicly or the first time they saw any interest or concern in their private stories from strangers.

On the other hand, during the workshop, I discovered the advantages of communicating physically rather than orally with the refugees. For example, we would often tap each other's shoulders, emphasising human relationships as part of our physical training. We used a special group exercise called "construction". The first performer goes to the centre of the stage, makes a pose and stays still. Then the second performer needs to come up with a different pose that creates a relationship with the first one. Each subsequent performer has to find a pose that connects with the former ones until everyone has constructed a "building of bodies". The refugees enjoyed this game a lot. I think it helped not only their understanding of bodily performance but also created a closer relationship among themselves as they had been strangers before.

Sun Weiwei: For the theatre piece *African Memory: Crossing*, did you discover new methods of dramaturgy due to multilingualism?

Wu Wenguang: In this work, every performer uses their own mother tongue, regardless of whether the audience can understand them. For instance, when the refugees perform their quarrelling on a small smuggler's boat (see Figure 11.1), they shout loudly in different languages, so the audience hears only a cacophony of human voices; the meaning is not important. In the rehearsals, the participants actively discussed what language should they use for this scene, but eventually they realised that at the time people cried in different languages. Therefore, we just kept the multilingual exchanges related to the actual experiences. Every language is equal in this show, just like every African refugee deserves a fair treatment despite their colonised and migrant identities.

In short, in *African Memory: Crossing*, the oral expression does not work as narration but more as symbol. Compared with *Reading Hunger*, this was a step forward. In the first work, the Chinese audience could still understand most of the recordings of the elders even if they talked in dialects. In this new performance, however, you would need to understand English, French, and several African languages. In my opinion, the languages and accents of the refugees are very profound by themselves. You can hear their French and English mixed with their mother tongues, and some even include Italian phrases because now they live in Italy. And because Mengqi and I are from China and the translator was Italian, you could say that the work covered three continents. For me, this is the most intriguing feature of creating a multilingual performance.

Figure 11.1 Ascoeddine Bacar, Moustapha Diallo, Nabieu Bangura, Romeo Francois. *African Memory: Crossing*. Directed by Wu Wenguang, Zhang Mengqi. June 30, 2017, Teatro Massimo, Cagliari, Italy

Credit: Photo by CCD Workstation/Wu Wenguang

Sun Weiwei: Given that memory is a core motif in both projects (FMP and the workshop with the refugees), what are your artistic strategies to use language to (re)construct these memories?

Wu Wenguang: One strategy we used in all of our performances was to convert oral memories into physical movements. As I mentioned in *Reading Hunger*, the young performers "translate" the words of the elders into movements. This synchronous reciprocity of words and movements is very efficient for us to translate a local or personal memory into a global emotion that everyone can recognise. In *African Memory: Crossing*, we applied this strategy as well, so you can see the African boys doing strange bodily actions when talking about their unhappy memories. Language is the bridge to (re)construct memory, but it wouldn't work without the traces of their physical experiences.

Another strategy we increasingly employ in our recent works is "searching the keywords". There are "Hunger", "Pain", and "Death" in the memories of the refugees, but, ultimately, we chose "Mama" as the most important keyword for *African Memory: Crossing*. We stumbled across this word during the conversations with the performers. Because the performers have barriers to understand each other, we had to find a common entry point to make this theatre happen. So the word "Mama" became the best choice, for it is crucially important for every human in the world, no matter whether they come from Guinea or Cameroon, Italy or China. This is how we found our opening scene. Before the lights come up onstage, you can already hear the rhythmic and strong singing of a group of African boys. It begins with simple lyrics: "Oh Mama". Gradually, you see them dancing, farming together as though they were in an African tribe. On the screen, behind them there are projections of photos of their mothers and family life in Africa. In this way, the word "Mama" serves as a key to the whole play: at some point, all the refugees talk about their mothers. Even if the audience cannot understand every word they say, when they hear "Mama" and see their evident emotions, they understand how nostalgic these boys feel and how far away they are from home.

Sun Weiwei: How many audience members attended this performance? What was the audience's ethnic and linguistic make-up? What were people's reactions?

Wu Wenguang: Over 100 spectators attended this production, two-thirds of whom were local Italians and one-third of whom were African refugees. Some refugees told us that this was a very valuable experience because it was the first time they could see that their suffering might serve as grounds for communication with others. Presenting their memories as theatre made the communication more interesting and profound than if it had merely been a report of their personal experiences (see Figure 11.2, one of the performers is replying to questions from the audience).

Figure 11.2 Bashiru Mohamed. *African Memory: Crossing*. Directed by Wu Wenguang, Zhang Mengqi. June 30, 2017, Teatro Massimo, Cagliari, Italy

Credit: Photo by CCD Workstation/Wu Wenguang

Sun Weiwei: Can you summarise briefly the most important lessons you learned from doing this project with the refugees?

Wu Wenguang: *African Memory: Crossing* was our first work in a multilingual and multicultural setting, so we learned a lot. However, to some degree, working with refugees is not essentially different than working with the elders in China. Although the reasons why people become refugees are very political, we concentrated on their unique memories as individuals more than the political or historical circumstances that made them flee. In the same way, we care more about personal stories of the Chinese elders than about the political reasons for the famine. However, compared with the Chinese elders, the refugees crave even closer personal connections with us. People often sympathise with them collectively, which makes them feel that they are not recognised as individuals. So we treated them as individuals and tried our best to make friends with them. For example, we became friends with a Cameroonian boy named Romeo Francois after we went to the beach with him and even played basketball and spent time with him and his friends. Our friendship provided a path for us to enter the African community, and it helped considerably in our communication in a way that went beyond language. I think that to create art from someone's memory, you need to understand the person first. On the other hand, compared to the previous works of FMP, since there were language and culture differences between us and the refugees, we needed to dig more into physical expressions and search for more intrinsic and emotional keywords in our dramaturgy.

Works cited

Lehmann, Hans-Thies. *Postdramatic Theatre*. Translated and with an introduction by Karen Jürs-Munby, Routledge, 2006.

12 Migration and the performance of colonial obscenity

Jean-Luc Raharimanana's construction of a theatre poetics

Alvina Ruprecht

When one asks Jean-Luc Raharimanana, a poet, musician, singer, and performer born in Madagascar (1967), to speak about his theatrical performances in France, he inevitably reverts to the horrors of the postcolonial period in his country of origin when his father was tortured under the Ravalomanana regime. Colonialism was officially over (Madagascar was under colonial rule from 1894 to 1960),[1] but in his work, Raharimanana refers back to a specific colonial massacre inspired by an anticolonial rebellion, *l'Insurrection des sagaies* (the "Revolt of the Paddles", 1947–1949), when thousands of farmers and local soldiers were massacred.[2] Both these events are at the origin of personal and collective trauma that have given fierce impulse to Raharimanana's creative writing, addressing the author's need to come to terms with both these tragedies.

Raharimanana arrived in France in 1989 after winning first prize in a national competition (sponsored by Radio France Internationale) in spite of the local censorship of his first play, *Le Prophète et le Président*. His family encouraged him to remain in France, as they feared punishment from the Ratsiraka regime. Staying in France, where his work as a poet and performer grew in popularity, Raharimanana realised the necessity of recovering the Malagasy culture of his country that had been obliterated by successive destructive regimes. His migrant status was unusual, however, since Raharimanana was a French national by affiliation—his grandparents and parents were of multiple origins, including French. French became his first language, whereas he had two nationalities: Madagascan and French. "I am a Malagasy of various origins, which include French, East Indian, a country in Africa (we don't know which one) and an Arabic country/culture, also unknown because our violent colonial history has interrupted our collective memory" (Raharimanana, correspondence, 2018). He raises this issue in his play *'47* when the actor from Madagascar (Sylvian Tilahimena), performing multiple voices representing his country, confronts the audience as the voice of the author. The actor wants to know why, if he is now living in Madagascar, a currently independent and formerly colonised country, it is so difficult for him to have access to his own family history and why his family and his country are still subject to the anger of repressive postcolonial powers. He implies that there is no difference between the two colonial periods and that his country has become an unbearable lie (Rarhimanana and Thierry 87–97).

In that destructive climate, Raharimanana also realised that his own national language, Malagasy, and the associated oral culture "inherited from the oral masters (mpikabary) who had transmitted their speech over generations, was being absorbed by a new culture unknown to us" (in Ruprecht 2017). This realisation forced him to cast his artistic gaze on the ruins of a precolonial culture and the oral traditions associated with it, defined by Laroche as *oraliture* (234).

Raharimanana's anger towards this situation became even stronger when in 2002 his father, a history professor and a former television broadcaster, was tortured and imprisoned in Madagascar. The writer realised that his own writing must henceforth be fuelled by the rage that emerged from the cruelty of those dictatorships whose sole aim was to annihilate the Malagasy population, no matter what the politics of the country happened to be.[3] These events triggered the next step of Raharimanana's writing: *Za* (2007), a novel in poetic prose inspired by his father's injuries . The jailers had broken his father's jaw and crushed his teeth; the text of *Za* (or *Je*) resembles a musical score in which the author transforms the sounds of the French language to create the speaking voice of a Madagascan whose mouth has sustained these injuries. Reading this text implied that the listener/reader had to rethink the phonology of Malagasy and work out new pronunciation patterns that effectively produced this new language.

Also in 2007, Raharimanana published his other work *Madagascar 1947*. Not intended for the stage, *Madagascar 1947* can be defined as an essay, an analysis, or an expression of the author's personal outrage over events pertaining to *l'Insurrection des Sagaies* that remained unspoken in his country. In this book, Raharimanana narrates survivors' testimonies in French and in Malagasy. He comments on the photos of those "subdued" (*soumis*) by the army in 1947, which he first saw in 2005 in the archives of Antananarivo: photos of starving individuals with swollen legs, skeletal bodies covered in bandages, and oozing wounds draped in filthy rags, barely able to walk, injuries clearly indicating that genocide had taken place in the country. Raharimanana relied on fragmented narrative forms that broke down the authority of the text and enhanced the presence of the master of kabary, who was able to dominate the crowd by the very act of speaking.[4] Determined to grasp the meaning of these events, Raharimanana became involved in an in-depth dramaturgical collaboration with the French director Thierry Bedard,[5] whom he met in 2007. This work confirmed Raharimanana's status as a migrant playwright in France, and it was an important event for both the writer and the director.

Raharimanana and Bedard: *'47*, the scenario and the staging

For the 2008 opening of *'47* at the Centre Culturel, Albert Camus in Antananarivo,[6] Bedard's theatre company Association Notoire provided background information about the uprising as the local audience knew very little about the events of 1947. When the show opened later in France, the printed programmes included additional information for the French audience about the history of Madagascar, reproductions of photos taken by the French occupying forces, and quotes from various commentators and information about Bedard's theatrical work, especially his cycle called *de l'étranger[s]*.[7]

Raharimanana cast a Madagascar performer to enact the many voices of the tormented inhabitants of the island, whilst Bedard brought in a white French actor to become the multiple voices of French history. These two performers, the lighting, the soundscape, and the photographic images of the massacre became the central elements of Bedard's staging. The photos that had finally been made available to the public in 2005 clearly showed the systematic destruction of the precolonial culture in Madagascar: its language, its collective memory, and its means of sustenance, as well as the profanation of the indigenous community and the eradication of its important rituals that more recent works for the stage have tried to recapture.

The links between personal accounts of torture and killing, published in the script of the play and testimonies of crimes against humanity, like those discussed by Hannah Arendt in *Eichmann in Jerusalem* (1963), were obvious (Perrone-Moisés, Clàudia and Mascaro 2017). Arendt speaks of "spontaneous testimony", creative forms of writing that are not "objective" historical accounts but rather examples of narrative memory which assume "artistic shapes" which help us to visualise the horror through the words of the victims (Wieviorka 96–97). Similarly, in *'47* the survivors' testimonies in Madagascar, recorded live by the author or presented in the form of letters read onstage, are linked to the photos in a series of 10 or 11 sequences, creating a Brechtian episodic structure with minimal narrative links between these independent "artistic shapes". Spoken by the two performers, the testimonies evoke multiple voices telling these tragic stories in the poetic rhetoric form of traditional storytelling. The audience hears these voices whilst different enlarged black and white photos are projected behind the actors and serve as background illustrations and elements of a set. They revealed thin, starving human creatures, their faces marked by sunken eyes and dark cheeks. The angry message of the migrant performer-poet became extremely clear as the spoken word often seemed to be contradicted by the cruelty of the background images.

One of the recurring themes of *'47* is the legitimacy of oral expression (Rarhimanana and Thierry 92). The French administrators questioned the legitimacy of the oral testimonies given by victims of the colonial extermination during *l'Insurrection des Sagaies*. These comments are revealing, especially when they are presented through the prism of the migrant gaze:

> Struggles for independence? Do they deserve to be included in history books? [. . .] those inaccessible written traces are only rebel legends that pass from mouth to mouth in whispers or in rumours spread by fear [. . .] How is it possible to believe such exaggerated adventures?
>
> (Rarhimanana and Thierry 88)

In these comments, one can hear echoes of French ethnologist Lucien Lévy-Bruhl's book *The Primitive Mind* (1922) that so influenced colonial thinking at the beginning of the twentieth century. Lévy-Bruhl proposed a systemisation of humans as primitive and civilised beings by defining primitive man as less capable of rational or abstract thinking. He suggested that "oral" language is a sign of a primitive society, an idea that confirmed existing colonial practices. Such depreciative references to "oral expression" have emerged in many migrant texts as clear testimonies of the racism that permeated the French colonial theories and practices.

In *'47*, Raharimanana and Bedard paid special attention to this historical injustice. They relied on Sylvian Tilahimena, the actor from Madagascar, and Romain Lagarde, a French performer, to transform the original text first to its theatrical form and then its filmed version. The cultural and ethnic differences of the actors found special resonance in this dramaturgical process because these differences symbolised the basic colonial conflict between the French and the Madagascans. As different ethnic voices they point continuously to the inferiority of the Malagasy language (Rarhimanana and Thierry 86). In one segment of the performance Tilahimena tries to describe himself as a colonised being who uses the euphemisms of the French language to avoid the vulgar reality of Malagasy. By trying to appear "cultured", he is deliberate in his pathetic attempt to show how the negative atmosphere of that colonial society diminishes the individual's sense of self-worth and produces people afraid to express themselves to the point of sacrificing their own language. The play shows the psychological effects of such demeaning behaviour by colonial and postcolonial administrators and makes the audience aware of the psychologically destructive relationship between those in power and those who are submissive to it. Raharimanana's revelations are the result of a nuanced critique based on the deconstruction of the relationship between local speakers and those in power who want to impose the colonial language.[8] Whilst keeping ironic distance, the strategy remains even more disturbing because the audience can identify the process very clearly.

Here the Malagasy-speaking victim ponders his level of speech:

> To say it more crudely, the colonized were supposed to evolve more quickly in contact with white people. To start with, we, the children of the colonies, had to give up our primitive languages—sorry! Our languages spoken by an inferior race—sorry! By Indigenous people—sorry! Our underdeveloped languages—sorry! Our developing languages of emerging nations. More scientifically, we have to give up our oral languages. (As if all language was not at first oral) our oral languages incapable of speaking about science, or discussing philosophy.
>
> (Rarhimanana and Thierry 88)

In performance, Bedard constructed a negative image of colonialism on multiple levels. He often relied on the absence of the text's narrative continuity, foregrounding the importance of the images and the secret photos that were released to the public in 2005.[9] He used these photos as props and as critical strategies to dismantle Lévy-Bruhl's teachings. Shown full-size upstage, these black and white images of terrified men, women, and children in rags became the accusing voices of the victims and the director's powerful critique of colonialism.

After this sequence on the primitive nature of oral language and implausibility of the testimony given in the Malagasy language, because primitive orality resembles rumours and whispering (Tabata in Malagasy), the background images fade and lights come up on Sylvian Tilahimena moving slowly downstage towards the audience, speaking directly to the public. He tells us that because he was forced to stop speaking the language of a "primate", he must now investigate his humiliation in a positivist way by slowly morphing into a chattering monkey, squealing, screeching, and chirping. He begins to scratch himself, leaping along the floor on all fours, in gestures of self-derision.

Such moments of physical performance are used to illustrate the result of problematic relations between the heads of state as Bedard, Raharimanana and their actors set up uncomfortable moments of male playfulness in which politicians themselves become clear objects of derision. Suddenly, the action shifts to 2005. Lagarde, the French actor, quotes French President Jacques Chirac's statement, made during his visit to Madagascar in July of that year, giving simplistic but well intentioned responses to the monstrous acts of planned extermination. At that time, since Madagascar was independent, Marc Ravalomanana, then the postcolonial President of Madagascar, accompanied Chirac. However, the poverty and suffering had not stopped and Ravalomanana appeared to be indifferent to the suffering of his own people. He stated that he was born in 1949, two years after *l'Insurrection des Sagaies*, and that as he was "not aware of the history of his country", he preferred to "look forward to the future" (Rarhimanana and Thierry 92).

Onstage, Tilahimena turns his back to the audience and giggles because the postcolonial president has just revealed his ignorance of his own history and his incompetence to rule the country. All this playful nastiness, taken from the French dailies from July 2005, confirms the migrant writer's desire to expose the fact that the contemporary world has inherited the colonial mentality without understanding its consequences. President Ravalomanana affirms he is not ready to discuss the past in order to avoid endangering his country's present good relations with France. At that point, the tall, stocky Lagarde (the voice of Chirac) drags the slighter more delicate Tilahimena (the voice of Ravalomanana) out in the middle of the stage to perform "the waltz of the presidents". Holding the young Sylvian closely, even pinching his butt, dragging him around the floor in a love-hate moment of high energy, Lagarde takes hold of Tilahimena, who assumes the terrified reaction of a prostitute forced to give herself to the powerful French politician. Quickly, the relationship disintegrates as the young man representing the voice of Madagascar dons the pants that the French actor has removed, and the younger actor sets off on a hot dance to the popular music of Salegy, making the French pants wiggle around his hips. The dance evokes Sartre's notion of the uneasy relationship (54–56) quoted in Raharimanana's text as "the striptease of our humanism" (Rarhimanana and Thierry 93), the text that originally appeared in the preface to Fanon's book, *Les damnés de la terre*. It mainly reveals our "lying ideology" as it shows the helpless president of Madagascar involved in this unexpected spectacle of dancing in someone else's pants. Raharimanana narrates his reaction to this spectacle by equating it to colonialism—a phenomenon of global lying, a perfect justification for pillage and exploitation.

> We are all accomplices, we have all profited from Colonialism. We are all monsters. And as a final moment, we are plunged into a hallucinatory reading of the tortures inflicted upon the rebels fleeing into the forest where the soldiers use biological weapons to create painful wounds on their skin, the proof that enormous numbers of human destruction and suffering that was inflicted on those armed rebels and how thousands were killed.
>
> (Rarhimanana and Thierry 96–97)

In performance, references to existing documents by such important voices as Fanon, Sartre, and Lévy-Bruhl are illustrated most concretely by physical actions and photographic documents. Raharimanana's dramaturgy is well served by a variety of sources; they are visual, intellectual, and corporeal. An audience consisting of different educational levels, different cultural backgrounds, and even those with no experience with theatrical performances at all can understand them. He breaks down all the barriers and thus illuminates the ugly realities he portrays.

In another segment, Sylvian pulls out a "precious document", a letter from the father of a friend, in which he provides an account of murderous events that took place in the forest during the uprising. In this sequence, Tilahimena's voice from Madagascar mutates into that of the father, as he reads that letter written in Malagasy. Lagarde places his hand on Tilahimena's shoulder in a gesture of friendship. This encounter between two bodies and two voices becomes a meeting of three persons: the father in the past and the two actors in the present, as they each exchange voices and languages. As Tilahimena reads the father's testimony of the 1947 uprising, Lagarde listens carefully as though he understands Malagasy and then offers a consecutive translation of this speech into French. This device produces a double reading of the same text in both languages in segments that follow each other. Both languages are heard fully, and both are given equal status in the acting space, which is important to elicit attention and sympathy. However, each "reader/translator" has a different reaction to what is heard and what is read. As Tilahimena speaks the father's words in Malagasy, his facial expressions appear traumatised. The French translator watches him closely, bowing his head in shame, pursing his lips, at times barely able to speak, especially when he has to translate the gestures of the French military as they push the still living "guardians of their idols" out of flying airplanes. The idea is to terrify the peasants with the sight of human intestines splattered over the earth as the bodies hit the ground. The destruction of these idols etched terror in the memory of all those involved because it also signified the death of their sacred figures, their sacred rituals. For European audiences, this scene brought up memories of political prisoners in Argentina in the 1970s during the "Dirty War" of the dictatorship.[10] Sharing the language of the stage with those audience members who also spoke Malagasy might also have created a deeper bond between the actors, their roles, and those not involved in the event, but it also resulted in the state representatives in Antananarivo cancelling the performance.

Ultimately, the voice from Madagascar reflects back on the first time the poet left his country as a result of persecution (1989) to become a migrant in France. The play comes full circle, closing with a final accusation levelled at "our own leaders" leaving the audience with a terrible sense of shame when they replaced the colonisers during that postcolonial era after 1960. They used the country's own language (Malagasy) to "strangle us,

[to] reduce us all to a state of infancy, underdevelopment, and stifled free-dom" (Rarhimanana and Thierry 99). The tortured voice of the poet returns to re-establish the absolute truth of his testimony:

> This was all true . . . the spears really existed, and whistled as they flew by, the bullets were devoured and absorbed and the cadavers danced their dance macabre. . . . As for me, I don't remember a thing except one date that burned as a red hot iron in my memory: March 29, 1947.
>
> (Rarhimanana and Thierry 99)

Having been forced to migrate and leave a nightmarish past, has Rahari-manana been able to reclaim even partially the memory of all that existed before the "colonial obscenity"? Perhaps not completely. But in his new country, where he is gaining popularity, Raharimanana is discovering new relationships with the stage and new performance strategies. New links with other countries are emerging, showing interesting postnational tendencies in his work. Nevertheless, the main impulse of his work, which is becoming even clearer in his more recent productions, such as *Ruins (des Ruines)* and *Sometimes Emptiness (Parfois le vide)*,[11] appears to be driven by the desire to recover the precolonial culture of his country that was destroyed by the leaders of the past. To avoid precise imitations of all that came from the past, he has located this recovery in a variety of current forms that add new meanings to the past, thus opening the results of this transfer between historical periods to new interpretations. This is no doubt the most interest-ing process of his migrant work. He presents texts in Malagasy to European audiences as orchestrations of sounds that harness extra linguistic mean-ings provoked by sounds which are not totally dependent on understanding the original language but that create poetic analogies based on physically attractive sounds. He sets up corporeal rituals suggesting a process of com-munication with a transcendent being, allowing the artist to forge a highly enticing relationship with all spectators. His live performance experiments have attracted a large following, opening doors to multiple festivals in France (Limoges, Avignon), thus epitomising the highly attractive results of this migrant adventure.

Notes

1 "Madagascar was under French colonial rule from 1894 to 1960. It became autonomous as the First Republic under the French constitution. The sec-ond republic extended from 1975 to 1991 under the regime of Ratsiraka who assumed power after the assassination of Ratsimandrava, appointed president of the Second Rupublic in 1975. Ratiskara returned to power in 1992. After the elections in 2001, Ratiskara fled to France and Ravalomanana became the next

president, remaining in power until 2009. It was under this regime that Raharimanana's father was tortured" (Raharimanana 2018)

2 All translations from French to English in the text are by the author.

3 Photos and other information concerning the inhuman treatment committed by
those who organized the quashing of the insurrection against French colonial
rule in 1947, *l'Insurrection des Sagaies* (1947), were officially sealed by the
state but were finally opened to the public in 2005. My sources for all photos
with written notes by Raharimanana come from reproductions in *Frictions #13*
(2008) 74–86.

4 In Madagascar, *kabary* signifies the art of rhetoric or a great speech held on special
occasions, such as the kabary of marriages or other ceremonies, family meetings,
the kabary to settle conflicts between individuals, clans or regions, or the public
kabary of itinerant theatre troupes. It also concerns daily life (Ruprecht 2017).

5 Thierry Bedard founded the Association Notoire in 1989. He spent much time
researching the countries of the Indian Ocean and collaborating with writers
from Mayotte and Madagascar .

6 The 2010 film version of '47 was filmed at le Théâtre de l'Échangeur, Paris,
directed by Thierry Bedard, produced by Koffi Kwahulé, coproduced by Axe-
Sud and France Télévision. I am grateful to Marie Pierre Bousquet for sending
me this excellent film.

7 In Bedard's words, this cycle of research relates to writing from around the world
which articulates the global order and disorder of human beings (Bedard 2018).

8 The writings of Etienne Balibar explain this colonial process in which language
is set in a complex dialectic between the colonised subject, deconstructed by his
relationship with the language of the coloniser, and an anthropological hierarchy
in the new society that would seem to be prolonged within the migrant context
of linguistic exchange, no matter what language is spoken.

9 Somehow, film and photography became the dominant discourses that contradicted the utopic pronunciations made by visiting French dignitaries on the island
who would come to address the local population and tell them how lucky they
were to be speaking a "civilised language" under the French colonial regime.
Curiously in this case, the oral expression of President Jacques Chirac of France
speaking in Antananarivo in July 2010, was not considered "primitive", even as
it was contradicted by the huge backdrops of enlarged black and white photos
of the dying human beings who were victims of these policies that foresaw the
complete extermination of an entire society (Rarhimanana and Thierry 92).

10 A former torturer interviewed by the *New York Times* testified that the navy conducted flights every Wednesday for two years, in 1977 and 1978, and that 1,500
to 2,000 people were killed. (Sims 1995)

11 http://capitalcriticscircle.com/parfois-le-vide-jean-luc-raharimanana-refait-le-
monde/

Works cited

Arendt, Hannah. *Eichmann in Jerusalem*. Translated from English by Anne Guérin,
Folio Gallimard, 1991.

Bedard, Thierry. *'47*, DVD filmed version, a coproduction of Axe Sud and France
Television, 2010.

———. "Un cycle de recherche lié aux écritures du monde où est énoncé l'ordre
et le désordre du monde." *Agenda Culturel*, 2008. www.agendaculturel.fr/notoire

Brecht, Berthold. "Dialectic and Theatre. Writing on the Theatre." Paris, *Editions Gallimard en collaboration avec l'Arche Éditeur*, 2000, pp. 391–503.

Laroche, Maximilien. *La double scène de la représentation : oraliture et littérature dans la Caraïbe*. GRELCA, U. de Laval, 1991.

Lévy-Bruhl, Lucien. *La mentalité primitive* (The Primitive Mind). P.U.F, 1922.

Perrone-Moisés, Clàudia, and Laura D.M. Mascaro. "Testimony and Crimes against Humanity from Hannah Arendt's Perspective." *Estudios ibero-Americanos*, vol. 43, no. 3, 2017, pp. 574–580.

Raharimanana, Jean-Luc. *Parfois le vide*, Unpublished manuscript, 2017

———. Personal email to the author. 7 May 2018.

———. "Photographic Documents with Hand-written Commentaries by J—L.R." *Frictions #13*, Fall–Winter 2008, pp. 74–86.

———. "Rano *Rano*." *Frictions #13*, Fall–Winter 2008, pp. 66–86.

———. *Des Ruines*. Vents d'ailleurs, 2012.

Rarhimanana, Jean-Luc, and Thierry Bedard. "'47. Text of the Stage Version Written by Bédard for the Théâtre Notoire." *Frictions #13*, Fall–Winter 2008, pp. 87–99.

Ruprecht, Alvina. "Parfois le vide; compte rendu." *capitalcriticscircle*, 4 Apr. 2018, http://capitalcriticscircle.com/parfois-le-vide-jean-luc-raharimanana-refait-le-monde.

———. "Writing beyond Language: Interview with Jean-Luc Raharimanana." *Critical Stages*, no. 16, 2017, www.critical-stages.org/16/entretien-avec-jean-luc-raharimanana-ecrire-au-dela-de-la-langue/.

Sartre, Jean Paul. "Preface." Fanon, Frantz, *Les Damnés de la Terre (The Wretched of the Earth)*. Éditions Gallimard, 1991, pp. 54–57.

Sims, Calvin. "Argentine Tells of Dumping 'Dirty War' Captives Into Sea." *The New York Times*, 13 Mar. 1995, www.nytimes.com/1995/03/13/world/argentine-tells-of-dumping-dirty-war-captives-into-sea.html.

Wieviorka, Annette. *L'ère du témoin* (The Era of the Witness). Plon, 2002.

13 Resisting the monolingual lens

Queer phenomenology and stage multilingualism

Art Babayants

My research focuses on the potential of multilingual dramaturgy where multilingual performers and audience members do not share a first language. *How does one approach such radical multilingualism from theoretical and practical perspectives?* To provide some insights, I will focus on the practice-based research project I conducted in Toronto, Canada, March through May 2015. The project, part of my doctoral thesis research, consisted of a six-week devising process with 12 mono- and multilingual performers. My collaborators and I were developing dramaturgical material primarily based on their own stories of language learning, accent acquisition or the failure thereof, traversing cultures, immigration, being the "Other", facing stereotypes, as well as rejecting and accepting novel cultural and linguistic norms. After six weeks of devising, we presented the dramaturgical material as a series of multilingual vignettes strung together without any linear plot. (For more on our devising process, see Samur 2017.) The "production," entitled *In Sundry Languages*,[1] was performed on two consecutive nights to an invited audience composed of multilingual speakers. No translation from one language to another was provided at any point.

Finding a suitable philosophical framework for this kind of artistic research proved challenging, as scholarly work focusing onstage multilingualism seemed to be dominated by semiotics and translation theory.[2] The main problem with the conceptual lens typically employed to carry out, as well as understand, stage multilingualism was that it was very much rooted in the monolingual modernist perspective that in turn has its origins in the concepts of nation-state and national (official) language.[3] A monolingual framework typically implies that a subject has one mother tongue, their "natural" language, so that any additional language is expected to be perceived and treated as foreign, not one's own. A monolingual framework typically also sees actors and audiences as almost invariably monolingual beings. In addition, it often assumes a single shared language—normally a language of power, for instance, such as the official language of a country or territory, a language that everybody is expected to speak and understand. (For instance, see Caplan's framework for multilingual dramaturgy 2014.)

In my research, I found that Sara Ahmed's conceptualisation of *queer phenomenology* (2006) can offer a fruitful theoretical groundwork to help scholars and artists reframe their monolingual lens, particularly when dealing with multilingual actors and multilingual audiences. Ahmed draws from the works of Husserl and Merleau-Ponty,[4] as well as a number of feminist philosophers, to indicate that our perception is not a function but rather an orientation (or direction) towards objects. For Ahmed, "it is not simply the object that determines the 'direction' of one's desire; rather the direction one takes makes some others available as object to be desired" (2006: 70). The key metaphor here is direction—re-orientating that one needs to do towards an object. Interestingly, Ahmed does not use the term "identity" (as in lesbian or gay identity, for instance); instead, she prefers to conceptualise identity as a set of repeated orientations (directions) that form a deceptively stable perception, which in turn begins to be read or understood as one's identity (see Figure 13.1).

To provide a telling example, Ahmed reflects on her own experience of "becoming a lesbian"[5] – i.e., ceasing her sojourn with a heterosexual partner in her "home" locale, moving to a foreign place, reorganising her life (and body), and beginning a "new life"—a queer life—which in her case means living with a lesbian partner. Ahmed explains that becoming oriented is a complex and often tedious process that starts with *disorientation* (2006: 107). Once a queer subject rejects being part of an invisible and compulsory heterosexuality, s/he has to go through disorientation, which is a process of parting with the repetition that essentially forms one's perception. The familiar will have to be rejected in order for the subject to become re-oriented.

In Ahmed's view, orientation and disorientation are not and should not be limited to sexual orientation. Whilst Ahmed starts with sexual orientation, in Chapter 3 of her *Queer Phenomenology*, she investigates how race (specifically mixed race) could be seen through the same philosophical lens (109–156). In her most recent volume, *On Being Included* (2014), she expands the queer phenomenological framework, focusing exclusively on race and how it is perceived in institutionalised settings. Being queer for Ahmed is not about being lesbian, even though being lesbian is also an inherent part of queerness—it is about orientating one's body against (or as

Figure 13.1 The process of orientating

she puts it—"around") the "compulsory" (127), be it compulsory heteronormativity or compulsory whiteness. Essentially, Ahmed proposes a resistive framework for understanding a queer subject.

Here, I would like to make a crucial pivot to multilingualism and multilinguals to elucidate how Ahmed's resistive framework can re-conceptualise the perception of multilingualism and multilinguals. Specifically, I would like to argue that multilingual subjects can demonstrate queer orientations, though they are not obliged to. As I mentioned earlier, in Ahmed's view, orientation and disorientation are not and should not be limited to sexual orientation. Ahmed extrapolates "queerness" to the concept of "orientalism" and investigates how race, specifically mixed race, could be seen as queer (2014: 123), whilst being white would be similar to Judith Butler's "compulsory heterosexuality" (90–91).

Following Ahmed, I propose to extend the metaphor of queer orientation from sexual orientation (which is a metaphor itself) to a multilingual speaker. In North America, we often live in a world of monolingualism that is commonly assumed and often institutionalised—in Butler's terms, compulsory. Thus, our perception is normally framed by a monolingual lens which trains us to assume the dominance of the mother tongue (in most cases *one* single mother tongue) and to treat a second language (L2) as an additional and typically subordinate language—the language of the Other. Just like with "racial otherness", L2 is there to "embody distance" (Ahmed's term). L2 is not something that belongs to an L2 speaker; it is a language and with it a culture and a body that a non-native speaker is never expected to possess. Instead, we are expected to be oriented towards our mother tongue and our L2(s) in very specific ways. Moreover, that kind of orientation can be institutionalised and internalised, for instance, through the endless questionnaires, forms, and censuses we have to complete throughout our lives.[6]

Ahmed writes, "It is through the repetition of a shared direction that collectives are made" (2006: 117). This is how communities are formed; this is how the perception of race is conceived, and I would argue that this is how monolingual (and/or monocultural) beliefs are instilled in individuals and society at large. Due to this compulsory "mother-tongueness"—a form of monolingual framework—a multilingual speaker must choose to "come out" as multilingual or pretend to exist, even temporarily, within the monolingual framework, just as Ahmed "came out" of a home culture that was ostensibly heterosexual and reoriented herself as a lesbian.

I contend that the queer phenomenological framework proposed by Ahmed is an epistemological key to creating stage multilingualism. In the case of *In Sundry Languages*, accepting the multilingual perspective meant accepting the possibility of playful engagement with different languages, not reducing performers to one single language (especially based on their accents or linguistic competence in a particular language), giving more space to minority languages, and learning to resist the need for direct access to the linguistic meaning. All these factors demanded the creation of a non-linear structure, very short scenes and an abundance of theatre styles rapidly changing throughout the show: a soft-shoe routine, a clown's monologue, skits, etc. More importantly, the dramaturgy of non-translation pushed us to find means to augment theatricality when the performance was not in the majority language—English. For instance, in the scene entitled "Kwin and Ozington", two multilingual performers Yury (a Russian and English speaker) and Sepideh (a Persian and English speaker) engage in verbal jabs, poking each other and making fun of the racist, ethnic, and gender stereotypes that Russian and Persian communities tend to have. What makes the dramaturgy of this scene interesting is that the intentional insults are only provided in Russian and Persian as aside comments, whilst the characters' responses to those insults are given in English:

SEPIDEH: Hi! My name's Sepideh.

YURY: Nice to meet you, Sepideh. I'm Yury.

SEPIDEH: Nice to meet you too.

Yury suddenly turns to the camera. Live feed: close-up on Yury's face.

YURY (*aside*): Сэпидэ, какое странное имя! Откуда оно, интересно?
    (*Turns back to Sepideh*). You look like Jasmine from Aladdin, the movie.

SEPIDEH: I'm Persian.

YURY: Oh, good for you. (*Aside*). Пержн—это Ирак или Иран? Или Сирия? А чо тогда это . . . шарф . . . хиджаб на башке не носит. (*Turns back to Sepideh*). So were you born here then?

SEPIDEH: My parents are not religious.

(Babayants 181)

As the scene was being devised, we decided to add a live video feed providing extreme close-ups of Yury's and Sepideh's faces. The asides to the audience eventually turned into asides to the camera and became an augmented version, almost a caricature, of facial expressions accompanying various racial and ethnic slurs. Whilst this augmentation produced more audience engagement (as reported in the post-performance audience surveys), it did not give those who did not speak Russian or Persian[7] any easy access to the linguistic (and often culture-specific) meaning of the actors' lines. Here is an example of a common audience member response from someone who spoke neither Persian nor Russian:

The languages they used were non-sense to me. But I followed their body languages, eye contact, expressions, tone of voice, intonation, sentence stress to guess what they were talking about.

(Babayants 234)

Essentially, the non-translation policy combined with the live video close-ups caused re-orientation—a need to read the untranslated languages differently. Those familiar with the languages reacted to the same scene differently. Here is a response from a Persian speaking audience member:

The part that Persian woman was talking to a guy in a party, because I'm familiar with language and culture and purpose of that woman.

(Babayants 235)

It was equally important for us also to challenge those who were able to understand more than one language. In another scene, Gloria, a fluent speaker of Cantonese, Mandarin, and English, delivered a monologue where each sentence was half in English and half in Mandarin:

I'm a quiet person. Because 我不喜欢废话，我只想把我的事情做好。In the Chinese world, my quietness is perceived as 傲慢. Apparently, my face just looks 傲慢 to them. Look at me, what do YOU think? In the Canadian world, 我的安静被看作是 shyness. In Canada, if you're not 大大咧咧, then you must be shy. 看着我，你觉得呢？

(Babayants 186)[8]

Throughout the scene, non-Mandarin-speaking audience members would have to re-orient themselves from reading the verbal meaning to interpreting Gloria's exaggerated gestures that accompanied each Mandarin segment of her sentences. Occasionally, Gloria's gestures would reflect the meaning incorrectly and the non-Mandarin-speaking audience would have to decipher why Mandarin speakers in the audience would react to her Mandarin lines in one way or another. Bilingual English-Mandarin speakers would presumably have the upper hand, as they could follow both languages and see when the non-Mandarin audience was being purposefully misled by Gloria's gestures. However, at the end of her monologue, Gloria suddenly removes this privilege of understanding as she delivers her final and most potent line in Cantonese, leaving the Mandarin speakers to re-orientate themselves as well.

In essence, multilingual dramaturgy that does not use translation can become *a queer object*, as it disrupts the notion of expected continuous access to the linguistic meaning. In other words, by limiting access, it creates distance and forces viewers to re-orientate themselves towards the presence of multiple languages. This re-orientation has the potential to be a highly enjoyable process, or it can be seen as violent if speakers of majority languages refuse to accept the loss of power that the non-translation policy may suggest (Karpinski 2017). One way or another, this potential for queer objects to be disruptive happens to be essential for Sara Ahmed, who asserts, "Queer objects might take us to the very limits of social gathering, even when they still gather us around, even when they still lead us to gather at a table" (2006, 24).

Notes

1 A quote from Thomas Kyd's *Spanish Tragedy*.
2 For more on this subject, consult Marvin Carlson. *Speaking in Tongues. Language at Play in the Theatre*. The University of Michigan P, 2006. Print.; Louise Ladouceur. Bilinguisme et performance: traduire pour la scène la dualité linguistique des francophones de l'Ouest canadien. *Alternative Francophone* 1, 2008, pp. 46–58. Web.; Nicole Nolette. *Jouer la traduction: Théâtre et hétéroliguisme au Canada francophone*. Les Presses de l'Université d'Ottawa, 2015. Print; J.B. Weisenstein. "Multilingual theatre in Taiwan." *Asian Theatre Journal*, vol. 17, no. 2, 2000, pp. 269–283. Web.
3 For more on this subject, consult Jan Blommaert. *The Sociolinguistics of Globalization*. Cambridge UP, 2010. Print.
4 E. Husserl and W. R. B. Gibson. *Ideas: General Introduction to Pure Phenomenology*. G. Allen & Unwin. 1931, Print; Maurice Merleau-Ponty. *Phenomenology of Perception*. Translated by Colin Smith, Humanities P, 1962. Print.
5 Ahmed's own term, which follows the Heideggerian classic of "dasein" and Judith Butler's idea of "turning" (Ahmed 2006: 15).
6 For example, the Canadian population census only recently began to differentiate between the concepts of "mother tongue" and "home language"; however, it still considers knowledge of other languages (presumably one's second languages) irrelevant, unless those languages are English or French—the official languages of the country (Linguistic Characteristics of Canadians, 2011).
7 The surveys asked the audience member to specify their language competences.
8 I'm a quiet person. Because I don't like bullshitting, I just want to get my shit done. In the Chinese world, my quietness is perceived as arrogance. Apparently, my face just looks arrogant to them. Look at me, what do you think? In the Canadian world, my quietness is perceived as shyness. In Canada, if you're not loud, then you must be shy. Look at me, what do you think?

Works cited

Ahmed, Sara. *On Being Included. Racism and Diversity in Institutional Life*. Duke UP, 2014.

——. *Queer Phenomenology: Orientations, Objects, Others*. Duke UP, 2006.

Babayants, Art. *"In Unknown Languages": Investigating the Phenomenon of Multi-lingual Acting.* Unpublished doctoral dissertation. University of Toronto, 2017.

Butler, Judith. *The Psychic Life of Power.* Stanford UP, 1997.

Caplan, Debra. "The Dramaturgical Bridge. Contextualizing Foreignness in Multi-lingual Theatre." *The Routledge Companion to Dramaturgy,* edited by Magda Romanska, Routledge, 2014, pp. 141–144.

Karpinski, Eva C. "Can Multilingualism Be a Radical Force in Contemporary Cana-dian Theatre? Exploring the Option of Non-Translation." *Theatre Research in Canada/Les Recherches théâtrales au Canada,* vol. 38, Fall 2017, pp. 153–167.

Kyd, Thomas. "The Spanish Tragedy." *University of Oregon,* Mar. 2007, http://darkwing.uoregon.edu/%7Erbear/kyd1.html.

Linguistic Characteristics of Canadians. *"Statistics Canada."* 2011, www12.statcan.gc.ca/census-recensement/2011/as-sa/98-314-x/98-314-x2011001-eng.cfm.

Samur, Sebastian. "'*In Sundry Languages*': Pleasure and Disorientation through Multilingual Melange." *Theatre Research in Canada/Les Recherches théâtrales au Canada,* vol. 38, no. 2, Fall 2017, pp. 236–242.

Index

Page numbers in italics indicate figures.

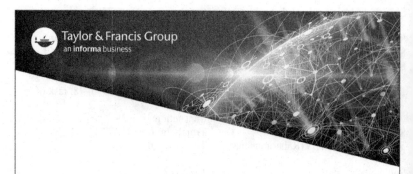

Printed in the United States
by Baker & Taylor Publisher Services